FILLIN' UP

mark Littleton

FILLIN' UP

Daily Fuel for High
Performance living.

MULTNOMAH
Sisters, Oregon 97759

FILLIN' UP

Published by Multnomah Books
a part of the Questar publishing family

© 1993 by Mark Littleton

International Standard Book Number: 0-945564-72-4

Cover design by Bruce DeRoos
Illustrations by John McPherson

Printed in the United States of America

Scripture quotations are from the *New American Standard Bible*
© 1960, 1977 by the Lockman Foundation; used by permission.

93 94 95 96 97 98 99 00 01 — 10 9 8 7 6 5 4 3 2 1

To
Carol and Gwen
Littleton

CONTENTS

INTRODUCTION

Fillin' Up

Christian living can often seem humdrum, colorless, even dull. Is this what Jesus promised when he said, "I came that they might have life . . . abundantly"? Is this all there is?

Yes, and no, and maybe. Depends on where you're coming from.

If you have no knowledge of God, no relationship with Christ, and no intention of getting to know the Lord, then *yes*—for you, this life is all there is, with possibly something far worse in the beyond.

If, on the other hand, you are a Christian and believe you know God but think there's really not much to it all, then maybe, just maybe, you will one day wake up and find out there is far more out there for you than you now imagine.

But if you're what I would call a zealous, go-for-the-gusto kind of Christian who isn't satisfied with easy answers and is willing to pay the price of real discipleship, then I can say to you in one final shout, "*No*, this is not all there is!" In fact, there's far more, every day, for those who will seek.

Hebrews 11:6 says, "Without faith it is impossible to please Him, for he who comes to God must believe that He is and that he is a rewarder of those who seek him."

Jesus said in John 10:10, "I came that they might have life, and might have it abundantly."

Paul cried, "I press on in order that I may lay hold of that for which also I was laid hold of by Christ Jesus" (Philippians 3:12).

And Peter counseled us, "Grow in the grace and knowledge of our Lord and Savior Jesus Christ" (2 Peter 3:18).

The Christian life, lived as God directs in the Bible, isn't easy. It's not always happy or adventurous. Sometimes it amounts to just slogging it away through the valley of the shadow of muck. But I've found it's always a *challenging* existence. And when the challenges are met head-on, the Christian life is *fulfilling* beyond measure.

Is that what you want? Then please read on. I want to live it up while I'm hear on planet Earth. I want to "go for the gusto." I want to get everything out of God's gift of life that my Creator intended. As you read, I think you'll see some of the ways a fuller life in Jesus is possible. Fill-up, anyone?

WEEK ONE

Making the Connection

MONDAY

Deep in the Pit

Holmes didn't know how he'd gotten into the pit. He'd been there ever since he could remember. His mother had been there. So had his father, brothers, and sisters.

It wasn't such a bad place. Jagged crags jutted up above him. The sun shone down and illuminated everything. Sometimes it was very hot, but a tree at the edge of the pit provided some shade. It wasn't too unpleasant.

He'd tried to climb out many times. So had his father. But it was quite impossible. The sides of the pit cut his hands and feet. When he *could* get a finger hold, he would nearly lose a fingertip or a toe before falling back in. There were other places where the walls were smooth and sheer as the slabs of shale that lay all about the floor of the pit. It was no use. Climbing out wouldn't work.

But Holmes wanted out. He hated the pit. It was desolate, lonely. For years now he'd been telling himself it was okay, he could make it. "Just cope," he said to himself. "Don't worry about it. No one else has it better than me." But something within him cried that life *had* to be better than this.

Then one day a man appeared at the edge of the pit. He looked down and spied Holmes instantly. "I see you're in the pit," he said.

"That's right," answered Holmes cheerlessly. "You know a way out?"

The man nodded. "I'm a great believer in the truths of the Buddha. They'll help you get out of the pit."

Holmes became excited. "What do I do? Please tell me."

The man said, "It's simple. You must overcome all desire. Follow the eight-fold path and you will break the endless cycle of karma. Your soul will be set free and you'll be out of the pit, even though your body will still be in it."

Holmes eyes narrowed. "My soul set free, but my body still here? What kind of nonsense is that?"

"It isn't nonsense. Just meditate. Eliminate all desire. Then your suffering will end."

The man turned and left.

Holmes snorted, "Well, I guess I can't lose anything by trying this stuff." He plopped himself down and tried to clear his mind. "I will think of nothing, do nothing, be nothing," he said. "I will end my suffering by eliminating all desire."

He concentrated. But as he did, it seemed his desire to escape the pit only magnified. The more he tried to eliminate desire, the more powerful it grew, until his mind seethed with a single passion to get out, to get away, to leap out of the pit. After several hours of struggle and failure, he gave up.

At that moment, he spotted another man passing by the edge of the pit.

Pumpin' Premium

One of the toughest things for Christians is dealing with these questions: "Why is Christianity true?" "Is Christianity the *only* 'true' religion?" "Is Jesus really the only way?"

To face the problem honestly, we have to lay some groundwork. First we need to agree that if something is true, it's true no matter what opinions others may have about it. For example, just because someone doesn't believe Jesus is God in the flesh doesn't mean he isn't. In other words, truth isn't a matter of opinion.

Second, we are in a world where truth is a battleground every moment of every day. If the Bible is correct on the issue of Satan and evil, then the devil and his cohorts are doing everything they can to deceive the world into believing that Satan's lies are the truth. Satan doesn't want us to believe the truth, because when we do, we defeat him.

Third, if we see someone being deceived, we should tell them. For instance, if we know the medicine cabinet contains poison and one of our friends is about to take that poison thinking it's aspirin, isn't it good and decent and right to point out the truth?

Satan is offering the world a horde of different poisons and every one of them is lethal. They are identified by names and slogans like these: "New Age," "an alternative lifestyle," "Do your own thing," "There is no God," and "God loves us regardless of what we do or believe." These lies are designed to keep us from discovering the truth.

As we start this study, we must reckon with the fact that we're in a war—a war for our minds and hearts. So check your weapons. Keep them at the ready. Living a truly Christian life isn't always going to be a walk in the park. But the effort pays long-term dividends.

Hit the Gas!

1. What is the major objection you or your friends have to the statement, "Jesus is the truth. There is no other way." What would you say to someone who believes it doesn't matter what path you choose to find God, so long as you choose one? _____

_____

_____

2. What do you know about Buddhism? What might you say to a Buddhist to help him understand the truth about Jesus?

_____

_____

_____

TUESDAY

Another Way Out?

"Hey!" yelled Holmes. "You have any ideas about how to get out of this pit?"

The fellow was bald, and wore a yellow robe. "Of course," he answered. "All you have to do is chant these words and everything will be okay: 'Hare Krishna, Hare Krishna, Hare Rama, Hare Rama.' Just say that about three thousand times a day."

"Why?"

"It'll make you happy."

Holmes slumped. "I don't want to be happy. I want to be out of this pit."

The fellow yawned. "Sorry. Our book doesn't say anything about pits. Just about how to be happy." He wandered off and Holmes once again was alone.

Suddenly a bearded man with a notebook stopped and gazed down at the hapless Holmes. "Can I offer you my services?"

"Who are you?"

"A scientist," he said, "a doctor of engineering."

"Fantastic!" said Holmes. "Can you engineer a way for me to get out of the pit?" The scientist looked around. "I think so. I've built such contraptions before. Let me see what I can do."

The scientist brought in a team of students who began putting together a marvelous piece of machinery. In no time the scientist had dropped it in by parachute. The machine came with a full manual and list of instructions.

"How do I work it?" shouted Holmes.

16

"Read the directions," said the scientist. Then he headed off down the road.

Holmes read. And read. And read. He tried this button and that lever. But nothing happened. Then he found the power cord.

"There's no where down here to plug it in!" he cried.

No one answered.

Holmes shouted again, but his voice only echoed. "Great!" he said. "I'm not only still stuck in the pit, but things are more cluttered up down here than ever."

He sat down and banged his fist on the ground. "I'll never get out of this pit."

Pumpin' Premium

Many people believe scientists can accomplish just about anything. Give them enough time and money, and they'll figure out a way to solve the problem.

But how do we solve the problem of death? Guilt? Salvation? Eternity?

Science can only go so far. Scientists can only study what they can see, hear, taste, touch, or smell. But how does one taste or touch God? How do we hear or smell demons and angels?

Like Holmes found out, science doesn't have all the answers. In fact, constant leaning on science as the end-all of life and existence can lead to trouble. During World War II, Nazi Germany became the ultimate scientific-materialistic nation. The Nazis performed research on human subjects in huge death camps. Their "scientific" beliefs, especially some of those centered on Darwin's ideas of natural selection and Friedrich Nietzsche's writings on a "master race" and the "superman," led to wide-spread suffering, the death of thousands of innocent people, and national self-destruction.

Science has limits. It can tell us much about the world and how things work or operate. But it can't tell us what is right and wrong. It can't show us the best course for our lives in terms of a career. And it can't answer our questions about eternal life and death.

Holmes was in quite a fix. But it really wasn't his fault. He was stuck. But his hope didn't lie in the machines of science.

Hit the Gas!

1. In what areas of life can we depend on science to give us the "straight dope"? In what areas *can't* it be depended upon to give us truth? _____

_____

_____

2. Why is science limited? What principles or truths govern it in this world? _____

_____

_____

WEDNESDAY

The Smoothies

"I can help," said a smooth voice. A man with a vast smile appeared near the edge of the pit. "If you think you can, you can!" the man added.

"What do you mean by that?" Holmes was intrigued.

The man spoke but his smile didn't move at all. "You must think in terms of possibilities, for all things are possible to him who thinks he can."

"What's the chance of me getting out of this pit?"

"Just decide in your mind that you can do it," said the smiling figure, "and you *will* do it."

"So what do I do now?" asked Holmes.

The man's smile didn't waver. "Plan. If you fail to plan, you plan to fail. But if you plan to win, your plan will win!"

Holmes felt a bit frustrated. "Will you please speak English? I want to get out of the pit."

"Plan your work and work your plan," said the man again.

"I don't *have* a plan," shouted Holmes. "And nothing has worked."

"Tut, tut," the man said. "Let me show you a few examples of those who have succeeded against all odds by using these principles I speak of." The man brought out three people who testified to the power of the principles. One had been poor, a second suffered from depression, the third had a poor self-image. All had succeeded by right thinking.

Holmes interrupted. "Look, my problem isn't thinking. It's the *pit*. I want to get out of it."

The man threw him a book, *Success Unlimited*, and said, "You can get others like it at the bookstore."

Holmes shouted, "I can't get to the bookstore." But the smiling fellow was gone.

Pumpin' Premium

Right thinking is important in many ways. If we don't think clearly and accurately about a problem, we can't solve it. If we don't have an objective understanding of a situation, we might act soley on the basis of our emotions and mess up everything.

But what about having a "positive attitude?" Isn't that a good idea?

Scripture speaks of having good, positive attitudes about many things. For instance, Paul told the Philippians, "Rejoice in the Lord always; again I will say, rejoice" (Philippians 4:4). Just a few verses beyond that is another: "Finally, brethren, whatever is true, whatever is honorable, whatever is right, whatever is pure, whatever is lovely, whatever is of good repute, if there is any excellence and if anything worthy of praise, let your mind dwell on these things" (Philippians 4:8).

Jesus frequently said we shouldn't lose heart but should keep trusting him about everything. What could be more positive?

Simply thinking positively, however, won't solve all your problems. Believing you can succeed goes a long way toward actually succeeding. But believing you can leap a hundred feet in the air won't make it happen. Pumping yourself up to do something that is downright impossible or beyond your abilities can lead to intense disillusionment.

The subject of death is another example. Telling yourself "I'll never die" won't make it so. And hyping yourself into believing that God will let you live forever because you were a "good person" doesn't mean that's what he'll do.

PMA (Positive Mental Attitude) can only go so far. And if it's not built on the truth, it's nothing but cheer-leading in quick-sand.

Hit the Gas!

1. What are some things that we should approach with a good PMA? (In other words, what areas of life are bettered by a healthy, happy attitude?) _____

_____

_____

2. Where does PMA fall down? What are its limits? How does it relate to being a Christian? _____

_____

_____

THURSDAY

A Different Kind of Helper

Another man appeared on the edge of Holmes's pit. He peered down at Holmes, then clambered over the edge of the pit and begin climbing down. Holmes watched with fascination.

The man found handholds and footholds where there was sheer rock before. As he drew nearer, Holmes noticed the man's back, bent and torn. And his hands and feet had great scars on them.

"He must often climb into pits," Holmes said to himself.

It was only minutes until the man alighted and stood before him. "Climb onto my back," he said.

He was about to protest, but the man's face was so utterly sincere that the hesitation and fear left him. He jumped on, gripping him tightly with his arms and knees.

The man began climbing. Holmes marveled as he watched him pick his way upward. He climbed smoothly—effortlessly from Holmes' point of view—but many times the man cried out in pain. When they reached the top, the man's fingertips were bloody.

Holmes hopped off and said with care, "Can I bandage your wounds?" The man held out his hands and Holmes made a dressing from some fresh grass and leaves. When he finished, the joy of being out of the pit struck him. He stood to suck in the cool air. "I can't believe it—*I'm out!* How can I ever thank you?"

"Just say it," he said.

Holmes laughed. "That's all? Just say 'Thank you'?"

The man smiled and nodded.

Holmes bowed. "Thank you." He paused.

Pumpin' Premium

The illustration of the man in the pit is just that: an illustration. Of course, if Holmes had been in an ordinary pit, he could have gotten out by many means. But the pit represents the human condition. We are all born lost, without hope and salvation. We all soon learn that life is a puzzle and the questions are many. Getting answers isn't always easy, and some answers are just beyond getting.

Holmes found himself completely without hope at the end, and that's precisely the way God wants us to be. All of us must reach a point where our own wiles, thoughts, ideas, and tricks fail to get us what we really need: Security. Hope. Forgiveness. A sense of being someone who is loved, understood, cared about. An inner conviction that death is not the end and that a hope of life beyond the grave is not a pipe dream.

That's what the Bible means when it says we are "lost." Each one of us must realize that nothing we *do* will ever win God's approval. No matter how hard we try, we can never be perfect. When we look at our lives and see all the dirt, muck, sin, and failure, only then do we truly have hope. That's when Christ can do something about our condition.

Notice that Jesus doesn't say a word; he simply climbs down into the pit. That's what Christ did—he came among us, lived, died, and rose again. We didn't ask for him. We didn't know to ask. He came because he knew we needed him.

Maybe that's where you're at right now. You're in a pit of guilt, fear, hopelessness, and insecurity. You know where you've been, and it isn't pretty. You know where you are, and it's worse. And you're sure you're headed for something that's no better.

If that's where you are, you're there because Jesus engineered it that way. He wants you to know that without him, you're lost. That's why he said, "Apart from Me you can do nothing" (John 15:5). We can't save ourselves. All we can do is let him come and carry us out on his back.

Hit the Gas!

1. Have you made a personal commitment to Christ? Do you see yourself as someone who was lost or is lost and needs to be found? Describe your feelings before you became a Christian. If you aren't sure you are a Christian, describe how you feel right now. _____

_____

_____

2. What do you think is the most important step for you to take today in relation to Jesus Christ? _____

_____

_____

FRIDAY

Giving Something Back

"How can I ever repay you?" Holmes asked the man.

The man smiled again. "You can't."

Holmes was startled by the man's blunt words. But suddenly he understood and said, "You're right. I *can't* repay you. I can only thank you."

Holmes gazed at the man, perplexed. It had been so simple. He asked, "But why did you do this? Why did you come down to get me?"

The man blinked. "Because I love you."

Holmes shook his head. "I don't understand."

"You will." The man got up and began walking away.

Holmes ran after him. "Wait! Where are you going?"

"There are other pits, other people."

"But what should I do?"

The man turned, his eyes piercing Holmes to the heart. "Follow me."

When he said it, Holmes's heart jumped. He stood there, momentarily staring back at the pit and the vast landscape before him. *I'm finally free. I could just go my own way,* he thought. *Why should I follow him?*

But something within him told him there was much more to this than just being free. *I've got to find out more about this man,* Holmes said to himself. He fell into stride beside the man.

Pumpin' Premium

Christ did something incredible for us when he came and died on the cross for our sins, and then rose again to life. His action made victory over death—and eternal life—possible. How can we ever repay him?

The fact is, we can't. God doesn't expect us to. He only asks that we believe, follow, and love him, giving thanks and appreciating him for all he has done.

Several years ago, my father told me and my wife we ought to think about buying a house. I said, "We're not in a financial position to be able to do that, Dad."

He answered, "Yes, I know. But I'm in a position now to help you. So if you're interested, let's discuss it."

The end result was that we moved into our own house less than five months later. Sometimes I ask myself, "How can I ever repay Dad and Mom?" I suppose I might be able to raise the money and give back to Dad what I owe, even adding interest. But my parents aren't as concerned about the money as they are that we be happy and enjoy our love and friendship with them. Repayment isn't what life is all about. Rather, it's loving and giving and sharing.

With Jesus Christ it's very much the same thing, except on an even larger scale. God doesn't want repayment; he wants a relationship of love, worship, friendship, and communication. All we can do is thank him and live for him in this world that is so bent against him.

Hit the Gas!

1. What is your deepest and most urgent response to Christ's salvation? What is your first thought after the idea, "I belong to him"? _____

_____

_____

2. What do you think is the appropriate response to God's love and goodness? Can you make such a response? _____

_____

_____

_____

WEEKEND

Truly in the Pits

"What's your name?" Holmes finally asked.

"I am who I am," he said. "But you may call me 'Lord.' "

Holmes nodded and began gazing about at the countryside around him. "It's so beautiful," he said. "I never knew it was like this." Suddenly he looked into the Lord's eyes and his mind seemed to fill with enormous thoughts, too great to contain. His heart swelled within him.

"This can't be," he said. "I might be crazy, but I'm beginning to think you're much more than a person who climbs down into pits."

"I am."

"But who *are* you?"

"I am the bread of life, the resurrection, the way, and the truth. But you can't understand all this now. You have to grow first."

Holmes bowed before him. "I suppose you're right. I want to learn from you, sir. And I will follow you. But how do I start?"

Suddenly a cry pierced the air: "Help! I'm in the pit!"

Holmes thought a moment. Then he leaped up. "That's it, Lord! I'll look for people in pits and you can come rescue them!"

The Lord laughed and motioned with his arm. "Yes. Do it."

Holmes ran in the direction of the voice. He found a man in a pit that was much like his own. He shouted to the man that help was coming. Then he looked toward the Lord and cried, "Over here, Lord. This man is desperate; he really needs you!"

Pumpin' Premium

I remember well those first days as a Christian. I wanted to tell everyone what I had found, *whom* I had found. It was a time of overwhelming joy.

Some of my friends, though, didn't understand this new enthusiasm and belief that I had. One of my best friends was getting married at the time and we decided to throw a bachelor party for him. The night before the wedding we all went out to a local drinking spot, and several of my friends proceeded to consume vast quantities of "liquid refreshment." Being a new Christian, I said I wasn't interested—even though I would had been prior to my conversion.

Several of the guys didn't understand my response. "Do you think it's wrong for *us* to drink because *you* don't want to?"

I told them it was completely up to them whether they drank or not.

One said, "What—do you think you're better than us?"

"No, not at all."

"You stand over there, all 'holier than thou,' treating us like we're rank heathen!"

I couldn't understand the problem they were having. I hadn't said a word to anyone about Christ. I hadn't even made a big deal out of not drinking. But later, one of those friends became a Christian himself. He told me, "We were all really convicted. We knew getting drunk wasn't right, and the fact that you could enjoy yourself and not drink just made us all mad. Like you had something we didn't—which you did."

Sharing your faith isn't easy. Many people don't see themselves as "lost," or as "sinners," or as being in a pit. We can't control how they respond to the message of Christ; that isn't our problem. We must simply find those in pits and let Jesus do the rest.

One of the greatest joys in Christian life is sharing the truth about Jesus. Seeing a person—who is lost in guilt, anxiety, and fear of death—come to Christ and leave all that behind is a remarkable privilege. As you get out there in your world, seek to discover those who are lost, and point them toward the Savior.

Hit the Gas!

1. Do you find sharing your faith easy? How do you tell if a person is in a "pit" and ready for the gospel? Is there a way? _____

_____

_____

_____

2. Write down the names of three friends whom you can begin praying for and eventually tell the news of Jesus. _____

_____

_____

_____

Week Two

Must We Live Under the Circumstances?

MONDAY

One Bad Situation

From his bedroom on the second floor, Terry Harmon could hear his parents talking quietly but angrily in the next room. His father had been acting strange lately—standoffish and easily angered sometimes, a little too polite and courteous at other times. His mother had confided to Terry that she thought his father was going through some kind of "mid-life crisis."

At seventeen, Terry was not naive about parental problems. He had many friends whose parents were divorced, and others whose parents had split up emotionally and were living with boyfriends or girlfriends. Terry recognized that life could be a mishmash of broken relationships. But he dreaded the idea of divorce or anything like it happening to *his* family.

He listened through the thin walls as best he could, but he couldn't make out the angry words he could hear on the other side. His mother's unmistakable hushed weeping came through clearly, though. Dad left the room. He went downstairs then out the door, closing it a little too carefully and quietly. Terry hugged his knees for a few interminable minutes, then stood and walked to the closed door of his mother's room. He listened. His mother continued to cry.

"Mom?" he said as he knocked.

No answer.

"Mom? Are you okay?"

There was a shuffle inside, then his mother was at the door. She had tried to clear up her tear-stained face but it was a botch, and her mascara had smeared.

"Yes?"

"I heard . . . well, you know. Dad sounded angry and then he left, that's all. Are you okay?"

"Yeah."

"Mom, you don't look okay."

Fighting to control her emotions, she said with a sigh, "I guess your father has decided to do something about his problem."

"What problem?"

"I'd better let him tell you." She sniffled into a tissue, then rubbed underneath her eyes. "I must look awful."

"You look okay."

"I'm sorry you had to hear any of that."

"Mom, I'm here whenever you need me."

"I know. Thanks. Get a good night's sleep, okay?"

"Okay."

She smiled weakly and closed the door.

Pumpin' Premium

A bad family situation can destroy your inner peace and joy like nothing else. It can leave you feeling insecure, fearful, harried, and unsure about the future.

The Bible repeatedly assures us that God understands our circumstances and can work in the midst of them. Romans 8:28 reads, "We know that God causes all things to work together for good to those who love God, to those who are called according to His purpose." And Jesus said to the disciples shortly before he went into heaven, "I am with you always, even to the end of the age" (Matthew 28:20).

But in the middle of a broken marriage, a desperate personal failure, or a devouring sin, a person may wonder: *Is God really with me? Does he care? Can he do anything about my situation?*

One verse that has always encouraged me is John 16:33— "These things I have spoken to you, that in Me you may have peace. In the world you have tribulation, but take courage: I have overcome the world."

God's peace and joy is possible even in terrible circumstances. To live above your situation is not a farfetched dream. God makes it possible through Christ's presence and power.

But notice what Jesus said: "In the world you have tribulation. . . ." He's warning us outright: This world is shot through with problems, evil, difficulties, suffering. He's not necessarily promising to change the circumstances, just to give us the resources in the midst of them to stand strong and firm.

Why not draw on that resource now, and ask God to give you his joy and peace in the midst of a tough situation you may be facing?

Hit the Gas!

1. What are some problems you're dealing with right now that make you feel low or worried? What steps can you take to work through them in God's timing and will? _____

_____

_____

2. From what you've learned, what would be a wise way of praying when hard times strike? Is God only interested in relieving us of the hard times, or is he more concerned about doing something else? _____

_____

_____

TUESDAY

It's Only Getting Worse

"I just think Dad should level with us," Terry said to his sister Carol at the breakfast table, after their mother went upstairs. Carol had cerebral palsy, but at sixteen she had many accomplishments to her credit, and she was hoping to attend college in two years.

"What do you think is going on?" Carol asked, in her hesitant, halting speech.

"I think Dad's being dishonest with Mom. Jerking her chain."

" 'Jerking her chain'?"

"You know, not telling her the truth—telling her stuff that gets her upset but which he thinks will make her feel better. Which it *doesn't*." Terry played with his cereal, not hungry at all. His stomach was a twist of knots. He didn't want to see his family fall apart. They'd been through some hard times together. Carol's cerebral palsy had been the greatest battle, just to give her the chance other kids had. But there was also the death of Mom's parents in a car accident last year. And years before that, Dad had suffered a bankruptcy. But they'd all weathered it together. What could be so wrong now that they couldn't face it together again?

Terry was not close to his mother or father, despite the sharing of common difficulties. They argued about nearly everything—they couldn't even agree to disagree. But lately, as Terry noticed his mother's quiet demeanor and her red eyes in the evening, he'd settled down; he decided to lay off until he had a fix on what was happening.

When Mom walked back into the kitchen, dressed for work, Terry asked, "What did Dad tell you last night, Mom?"

She turned away and went through the motions of putting bread in the toaster. But from the rear her shoulders looked hunched, as if someone had let the air out of her.

"Mom, just tell me, please. Be honest. That's all I ask."

She turned around. "All right. Dad said he doesn't love me anymore and hasn't loved me for several years."

Terry swallowed and stared at his mother's eyes. She didn't wince or cry this time.

"He's been leading up to it for months, I guess. I probably should have seen it coming," she added.

"What's he going to do?"

She looked at her hands, then sniffled. Soon she was weeping again. "I don't know."

Terry stood and Carol was next to him immediately. They both hugged their mother and spoke tenderly to her. But Terry prayed that this wasn't really the beginning of an end he didn't want to face.

Pumpin' Premium

An artist once wanted to paint a portrait of "perfect peace." He spent months, even *years* thinking about the theme; finally he was ready to paint. What he produced wasn't a meadow on a calm day with cows lazily chewing their cud in the foreground. It wasn't a picture of a business meeting with everyone smiling. It wasn't even a classroom with a boy in the front holding up a giant 'A' as his grade for the day.

No, the artist pictured a raging storm at sea. The waves crashed over the rocks like vipers spitting white venom. The sky was stark black. You could almost hear the howling wind as you looked, and feel the wind-driven spray as it lashed your cheeks and eyes.

How was this perfect peace?

One might not notice, but down in a lower corner was a completely different scene. A small bird, hidden deep in a recess among the rocks, sat quietly on a nest. Her eyes didn't dart about in terror. She nestled deep down into her feathers and even seemed about to fall asleep.

Perfect peace and joy is not living it up when things are going well. No, real peace—the kind that works and lasts—must remain unchanged even when the storm rages outside.

How is that possible? It can happen this way only for the person who knows the *master* of the storm. When we realize that God is in control of even the winds and the sea, then we can have perfect peace. Because then we know that he loves us and will take us safely to his heavenly kingdom. Like Paul told Timothy when he faced the ax that would ultimately lop off his head: "The Lord will deliver me from every evil deed, and will bring me safely to His heavenly kingdom" (2 Timothy 4:18).

Hit the Gas!

1. How confident are you that the words of Scripture are true? What verses do you know that seem to contradict the way things happen in the world? How can you reconcile God's Word to your situation in life? _____

_____

_____

2. What problems give you the greatest doubts about God's love? What can you do to become free of doubt in the midst of bad circumstances? _____

_____

_____

WEDNESDAY

Day of Reckoning

Things were quiet for three months. Terry's father did everything right. He was courteous, opened doors for his mother, spoke quietly, kept his temper in check. He took her out to dinner several times, but Mom wouldn't reveal what they'd discussed.

Then one morning as his father walked in to breakfast, Terry stood and confronted him. "What are you doing, Dad? Just give us the straight dope. I'm tired of seeing you pretend."

"What do you mean, Terry?"

"Do you love Mom?"

Mr. Harmon blinked twice, then looked away. "That's none of your business, Terry."

"It *is* my business. It's *my* mom and *my* family. Do you love Mom or not?"

His father clenched his jaw. His cheek twitched. Terry was as tall as his father, and certainly stronger. As a member of the wrestling and track teams, he was in good shape. He and his father had never fought, but the fury inside him was building.

"Just spit it out, Dad. I want the the truth."

"Don't be insolent with me, young man." For a moment their eyes met.

"All I'm asking for is honesty, Dad. Do you love Mom?"

His father looked away. "I don't know."

"You don't know! What kind of answer is that?"

"I don't know. That's the best I can do right now."

Pumpin' Premium

Few things in life are more upsetting than watching your parents' marriage disintegrate. When we're young and living at home, much of our security is tied up with the security that Mom and Dad give us. But if they're constantly fighting and on the verge of splitting up, we naturally wonder, *What will happen to me? Who will I live with? What about college? What about Christmas and birthdays?*

Researchers who have studied young people going through their parents' divorce find that the children often feel it's their fault. They reason that if they had just been better kids, their parents wouldn't have failed in their marriage.

In some situations, a parent may even blame the kids. "If you weren't such trouble, your Mom and I would get along." Or, "If we didn't have you around, it would be a lot easier."

Statements like these amount to virtual abuse. But they happen.

And yet, even in *these* circumstances, young people can find hope in the midst of their distress. God says he will be a "father to the fatherless," and will stand with the orphan. He will be with such people in a special and everlasting way because of their pain.

How do you find peace and joy with God even when things are terrible and seemingly out of control?

In Philippians 4:6-7, Paul says, "Be anxious for nothing, but in everything by prayer and supplication with thanksgiving, let your requests be made known to God. And the peace of God, which surpasses all comprehension, shall guard your hearts and your minds in Christ Jesus."

This isn't a formula which, if followed correctly, will result in an emotional peace that no one can understand. Rather, it's Paul's directive to people who were persecuted, fearful, and worried about their friends in prison. Paul was encouraging them to refuse to let anxiety control them. Rather, when fear strikes, they were to pray and give God specific requests about their circumstances, while at the same time giving him thanks that he is there and in control and able to bring good out of bad. It's through such faith and confidence that real peace comes—a peace we may not even understand, and others will marvel at.

Warren Wiersbe said in his book, *Be Joyful*, "Rejoice at what God is going to do instead of complaining about what God did not do."

Remember above all: Christ is coming; we'll one day live in a new world and time. Christ will reign there, and we will reign with him. That was the outlook of the early Christians; it's what gave them the power to face the lions and burning stakes.

Hit the Gas!

1. What are your greatest fears? How can you turn them over to Christ today? _____
_____
_____

2. What does Scripture say God will do? How does thinking about and relying on that truth help in the midst of hard times?
_____
_____
_____

THURSDAY

Little Hope of Recovery

Over the next few weeks, Terry's father was quiet and courteous. Even stiff. He went out every night. No one knew where. But at family gatherings—the Fourth of July, an aunt's birthday party—he kept up the show. Terry was outraged. But his mother wouldn't give him more information, even though she cried nearly every night in her bedroom when his father went out.

It felt to Terry as if everything was leading up to Carol's birthday in late July. One morning shortly before the event, Terry sat alone with his mother in the living room. "Mom, is Dad leaving?" he finally asked after several minutes of small talk.

She nodded reluctantly. "I think so."

"After Carol's birthday?"

"I think that's what he's waiting for."

"You know Carol will be devastated."

"I know."

Terry decided not to press it further. Carol's birthday went as expected. Everyone was in a celebratory mood except Dad, who was stiff, too perfect, too in-control. Terry said nothing, but the next morning, Saturday, at breakfast, his father announced he was going out to run some errands.

That evening he returned, packed his bags, and called the family into the living room. Carol was already sobbing. Terry stood stone-faced behind his mother as she sat on the couch, fighting to hold back tears.

"Your mother and I are getting a divorce," his father said abruptly. "I'm leaving. You will live with your mother and I will pay for your education." He picked up his bag and started for the door.

Terry leaped in front of him. "Is that all?" "That's all, Terry."

Staring at his father, Terry fought back waves of nausea, anger, and a strange, swelling unbelief.

"This is the way it ends? You're just going to leave? Not even an 'I'm sorry'?"

"I'm sorry, Terry. Now I've got to go."

His mother burst into tears, and Carol began to get hysterical. Finally, Mrs. Harmon said to Terry. "Let him go, honey. There's nothing we can do about this."

Pumpin' Premium

There's a story about an accountant who got tired of numbers and decided to become a truck driver. The idea of sitting on top of a huge eighteen-wheeler and all that diesel power excited him. When it came time for him to take his final test to be approved to drive such a truck, an official sat him down and said: "There's only one question. You've just come over the crest of a two-mile-long hill. A hundred-car train has just started into the crossing two miles below. You decide to slow down and hit the air brakes. But they're gone. They're completely shot. You go for the emergency brake and it's broken. You try to shift down, but the shifter is stuck in ninth gear. You're gaining speed now and the train is steaming across the intersection. It's less than a mile away. Your partner, Charley, is asleep in the bunk above you. What do you do?"

The accountant thought for a minute or two and finally said, "I wake up Charley."

"Why?"

Flashing a big grin, the accountant said, "Because Charley's never seen a real bad train and truck wreck."

Tall tales aside, life can seem like that sometimes. All you can do is step back and watch the turmoil. You have no power to control events. You can't change anyone.

No one?

That isn't quite right; there *is* one person you do have some control over—*you*. We can choose to have a God-honoring attitude and outlook even in the midst of deep stress. On "Good Morning America," Jimmy Dean once said, "I can't change the direction of the wind, but I can adjust my sails to always reach my destination."

The beautiful truth for all Christians is that we're not alone: "Greater is He who is in you than he who is in the world," John says in 1 John 4:4. We may feel deserted, but God assures us, "I will never desert you" (Hebrews 13:5). We may think all looks hopeless, but Christ calls out of the darkness, "I go to prepare a place for you" (John 14:2).

Joy is possible even in the midst of great trouble, if we'll only seek it.

Hit the Gas!

1. What comfort does the idea "God is in charge" give you? Is it true? And if it is, why does it so often look like he's *not* in charge? _____

_____

_____

2. Which Scriptures do you know that can help calm stressed nerves? _____

_____

_____

FRIDAY

It's Over

The cold finality of it all hit Terry two years later when the courts pronounced Mr. and Mrs. John Harmon divorced. Terry had gone to the hearing. Carol hadn't attended it because she was still too upset about the breakup of her family.

That night Terry, Carol, and their mother sat at the dinner table in a morose, pained silence. Terry noticed that his mother was no longer wearing her wedding ring. Working up his courage, he finally said, "Mom, you took off your wedding ring today."

"Yes, I did." She spoke to her plate, but then looked up, her eyes level with Terry's. Carol sniffled, and Terry reached over and squeezed her hand.

"Well, I guess it's just us now," he said tightly.

"Your father will see you, honey," Mrs. Harmon said. "He cares about you still. He still loves you."

"Don't defend him, Mom."

"I'm not defending him."

"He's destroyed everything."

Mrs. Harmon reached across the table with her left hand and Terry again noticed the emptiness of the hand without the ring; it was as if an organ had been ripped from his mother's body. He took the hand and she squeezed. Then she took Carol's hand.

"We'll live through this," Mrs. Harmon said. "God will be with us."

"Yeah, like he was with us when Dad left?"

"God didn't make Dad leave, honey. And God *does* work all things for good, even bad things."

Terry fought the desire to cry, but his eyes misted. He looked into his mother's eyes and they were wet. He wondered for a moment if he believed it anymore, with the father who'd taught this very principle to him now gone.

That night, Terry walked into Carol's room and talked quietly with her. He concluded, "We need to do something for Mom that will help make us all feel like a family again. So think about it, okay?"

Pumpin' Premium

Frequently, God doesn't change circumstances; he doesn't make things turn out like we wish they would. A divorce occurs, and a family disintegrates. Dad or Mom leaves and doesn't come back. Or a friend dies.

Does this make you doubt God's goodness, love, and care?

Sure it does. We don't understand. If God really is sovereign, if he really can bring good out of bad, then why does it seem like there's so much bad and so little good? Especially in *my* life!

Part of it is perspective. Perhaps one major thing has gone wrong in your life, but what about all the other elements of it that are right?

But the more important consideration is that God hasn't promised to make everything in life good, happy, and hopeful. He only promises to make good happen in the midst of the bad. He promises that he'll get us safely to heaven. And he promises that nothing in this world can separate us from him.

Terrible circumstances become much less a problem when we realize two things. First, this world is a battleground. A war rages even now between heaven and hell, and we're in the middle of it. In a war, terrible things happen. Our world, for all its grandeur and glory, is nothing but a battlefield in which people get hurt, maimed, broken, and killed. No one will get out of this mess alive.

Second, God assures us he has *already won* the battle, and one day it will all be over. This world is only our temporary home. Jesus will come again. We are headed for glory forever with him. That is the hope God wants us to keep our eyes fixed on.

Hit the Gas!

1. How does the hope of heaven strike you? Is it enough? Is it important? How does it look next to your goals and hopes in this world? _____

_____

_____

2. Do you need to realign your focus? Have you gotten caught up in the things of this world so much that you've forgotten your destiny? What can you do now to readjust that focus?

_____

_____

_____

WEEKEND

A Light in the Darkness

Six months later, Carol led Terry through the mall to a jewelry store. "Remember how Mom's hand looked so empty without her wedding ring?" she said.

"Yeah." He was surprised she'd noticed too. But she was always sensitive like that.

"This place makes a special ring. I'll show you." Carol took him to the counter and they looked at the ring—a gold band with a large birthstone in the middle and two smaller birthstones on the sides. It was beautiful. "We can put Mom's in the middle and each of our birthstones on the sides. She can wear it on her wedding-ring finger."

Terry knew it was right. It would be hard to earn the money needed to buy the ring, but they both decided they had three months to do it and it would be one mountain they would climb together.

Three months later, on their mother's birthday, he and Carol presented the ring. Their mother was overjoyed and overwhelmed. She cried, but they were good, joyous tears.

As they all hugged and laughed over the sparkle of the three gemstones, Terry said, "There's something else I wanted to tell you, Mom. Carol, too."

The two women looked at Terry. He felt a bit uncomfortable at first, but as the words sprang into his mind, he said with rising confidence, "Remember how you said God works things for good, even bad things?"

His mother smiled. "I hope I still believe it."

"Well, our situation *has* worked for good," he said.

Carol smiled, but Mrs. Harmon just stared at him with some amazement.

Terry said, "It's brought me closer to you and Carol. For a long time we argued and fought and had lots of problems. But you know, we haven't had a real fight in months."

Mrs. Harmon smiled as a tear slipped down her cheek. Terry gripped her and Carol's hands. "It's not the best situation, but at least God's still working in our lives."

"Yes," Carol said, "and we can count on that forever."

Pumpin' Premium

Joy is a hard commodity to come by in our world of problems, difficulties, distress, and despair. You need only to read the newspaper to see situations that stagger the understanding and rob you of hope.

It's our personal difficulties that most thwart us. Even prayer, a determination to hold onto the promises of God, and a commitment to Christ can sometimes seem to do little more than mock us. If our bad circumstances remain the same, why should we believe God really is bringing good out of bad?

One thing we must do is give God time to work. Just as terrible circumstances are often the result of many smaller bad decisions, acts, and attitudes over a long period of time, so God can't and doesn't make a miracle happen just to get us out of a tight spot.

Also, we need to recognize that God is not just out to make us happy in this world. Sure, he'd like us to enjoy life and the good things of his creation. But Jesus himself was "a man of sorrows and acquainted with grief." If we think this world is all about happiness, fun, games, and good times, we are missing an important point of Scripture. Jesus "learned obedience from the things which he suffered" (Hebrews 5:8). In other words, God was more concerned that Jesus obey than he was that he "feel good."

But what does obedience do for us? When we obey, we experience true joy. It's then that we can understand God's blessings in our lives.

Senator Sam Ervin, made famous during the Watergate scandal of the 1970s, said, "Religious faith is not a storm cellar to which men and women can flee for refuge from the storms of life. It is, instead, an inner spiritual strength that enables them to face those storms with hope and serenity. Religious faith has the miraculous power to lift ordinary human beings to greatness in seasons of stress. Religious faith is to be found in the promises of God."

Out of suffering and pain come obedience. And from obedience springs joy, love, peace, and all the fruits of the Spirit. James said it best: "Consider it all joy, my brethren, when you encounter various trials, knowing that the testing of your faith produces endurance. And let endurance have its perfect result, that you may be perfect and complete, lacking in nothing" (James 1:2-4).

Welcome hard times as a means of personal transformation. If you let Christ mold you, you will emerge from trials a stronger, more resilient, and more joyful person than ever before.

Hit the Gas!

1. Look at James 1:2-4. What does this Scripture say is the secret to facing trials with joy? _____

_____

2. Consider Paul's words in Romans 5:3-5. What was Paul's secret for rejoicing in troubled times? How could he do that? What did he see beyond his personal trial? _____

_____

Week Three

The Hope that Keeps on Hoping

MONDAY

Father and Son

Judd Lezerian sat on the bench watching Craig Morgan dribble the ball up the court. Being second string was hard. But knowing his dad was in the stands was comforting—even though his dad was blind. For three years now, Judd had been the only guy on the basketball team whose father attended every game. It was a funny story around the locker room—Judd's Dad was so loyal, yet he couldn't see a thing.

"I mean, he can't even see you sittin' on the *bench*," Judd's friend Lee Harrison often said.

But Judd had been working hard. He and Craig Morgan had battled it out in scrimmages and practice and Craig had edged Judd out of the starting position by only one free throw. Judd had gone twelve for twenty; Craig hit thirteen of his shots. Otherwise, Coach Pellerend said, "You guys are about dead even."

Tonight's game was the first Judd might get to play in. If Craig messed up or something, that is.

Not that Judd wanted him to mess up. Or get hurt, or anything else. He wanted to win the right to play fair and square. But sitting on the bench was hard.

"Put Lezerian in!" yelled a voice from behind the players' bench. It was his sister Suzy; she came to most of the games too.

Judd just sat still and straight, hoping his team would get ahead and he'd be able to play a few minutes.

The whistle blew. Foul. The ref raised his arm, ran over to the officials' bench, and said, "Foul on sixteen!"

It was on Craig Morgan. Craig rarely fouled, but this was his third tonight.

A second later, Coach Pellerend called out Judd's name. "Lezerian, get up here."

"Go, Lezerian!" Judd heard his father's strong voice roar out. One thing Judd could count on was that his dad would *hear* everything, even if he couldn't see it.

Pumpin' Premium

Years ago, there was a song by James Taylor called "Fire and Rain." In it he spoke of his love for a girl he'd met at a psychiatric facility. Taylor fell in love with her and began to recover from his illness as his love grew. But the girl committed suicide and their love was never complete. In the song, Taylor cries:

"Won't you look down upon me Jesus,
You've got to help me make a stand.
Just got to see me through another day.
My body's aching and my time is at hand;
I won't make it any other way."

Some of us who became Christians in that era wondered if James Taylor had become a Christian too. To this day I don't know. Yet the words of his song often ring in my mind. With all our science, with all our inventions and material wealth, there is still much despair and heartache in our world. We have not found a way to make every story turn out for the best in the end. The "happily ever after" that our fairy tales end with are just . . . well, fairy-tale endings.

But for the Christian, hope—the kind that looks to another day, a better world, a place of peace and joy and goodness—sticks with us. It makes the troubles of this world bearable. And it makes "hanging in there" worthwhile.

I don't know about you, but I have a lot of hopes. Many of them, I know, will never be realized till Jesus comes again. But each one of them keeps me looking forward to that day.

Hit the Gas!

1. What do you look forward to and hope for? What do you wish will happen in your life this year? This decade? List three things you believe could come to pass but which you know only God could do? _____

_____

_____

2. Read Romans 8:24-25. What does this passage teach you about the nature of hope? How is it that hope that is seen is *not* hope, but hoping for what we can't see, is? _____

_____

_____

TUESDAY

Playing for a Blind Man

"Time, ref," Coach Pellerend called out. The coach called Morgan over. "I'm putting in Judd. You have three fouls, Craig."

"Yeah, I know, coach. I'm off tonight."

"That's okay. Take a seat and rest."

"Judd!"

A split second later, Judd stood beside the coach. "Watch that number twelve, the guy who Craig's been covering. He's pulling fouls whenever he can."

"All right."

"GO, LEZERIAN!" Judd's Dad yelled as the boy ran out onto the court amid much cheering from the stands.

It had been a tough half up to this point. With just two minutes left before half-time, Judd wouldn't have a chance to get in much before the break. As a six-two forward, Judd set up posts, ran some picks for the guards, and was alert for their center's rebounds. Usually their center would wing the ball up if he had a chance, or fire it out to one of the forwards. Judd ran the plays expertly. After forty seconds of play, he had his first chance at a shot.

It came on a steal by Jeremiah, a guard. Jeremiah caught the Coldwell team off-balance, and he rocketed down the court. Judd, being fresh, took off with him. Only two opposing players managed to keep up with them. Judd ran parallel to Jeremiah, outside.

Jeremiah didn't have a chance to shoot. But he was an excellent passer: He whisked the ball behind his back to Judd, who was coming in on the left; he was in position for a lay-up. Judd was tempted to go for a dunk. He was a good jumper and could do it easily enough.

But this was not a crowd-pleasing game. They had to win it to get into the finals.

The pass was right on. Judd dribbled twice, then went airborne. He laid the ball up against the left backboard. It sank in for two.

Judd got his only other two-pointer on a single-hand feint-and-leap shot from the point. It sank in the final seconds of the first half. The crowd roared. Judd heard his dad's voice in there and wondered if his father could visualize what had happened.

Pumpin' Premium

Emily Dickinson wrote, "Hope is a thing with feathers that perches in the soul."

Nice picture. Imagine Judd playing basketball, with his blind Dad cheering in the stands behind him. Many families in our world today are not close. Too few have a mom and dad in the same home, let alone a dad who goes to see his son's games.

Even with his blindness, it's obvious that Judd's father cares about his son. He goes to "hear" a good game, and to exercise his own brand of hope—that his son will get a chance to play.

In fact, as you look at this story, you see hope all over the place. Judd hopes he'll get into the game. Then, once in, he hopes that his shots will be true and he'll score, and that his father will somehow be able to be part of it all despite his blindness. Perhaps deep down, Judd hopes that one day his father would be able to see again, too.

Much of life's quality depends on our level of hope. Do we have realistic, gutsy, expectant hopes that have some possibility of coming to pass? Are we energized by the force of grandiose hopes for our future, family, and world?

Consider some of the hopes God has put into our souls, according to the Bible:

- "The hope of eternal life"—Titus 3:7.
- "A helmet, the hope of salvation"—1 Thessalonians 5:8.
- "Love . . . hopes all things"—1 Corinthians 13:7.
- "Hope does not disappoint"—Romans 5:5.
- "Through . . . the encouragement of the scriptures we might have hope"—Romans 15:4.

How are your hopes? Having "something around the corner" is "the one thing that gives radiance to everything" else. So said G.K. Chesterton, a mystery writer of a century past who was also a fervent Christian.

Hit the Gas!

1. Why do you think love "hopes all things"? What is the principle behind that statement? _____

_____

_____

2. Have you ever felt hopeless? Why? When? What gave you new hope? Why? _____

_____

_____

WEDNESDAY

A Chance to Start

Morgan went in for the second half and played the rest of the tight game. But with four points in only two minutes of playing time, Judd was a high scorer. The coach said to him as they exited the court, "You do well in practice this week, I might start you on Wednesday."

Judd burned to tell his sister and father, and when he met them after showering and dressing in the locker room, he was brimming with excitement. "Coach said I might start next week if I play well in practice," he said.

"You can do it," his father said, clapping him on the back. "Hope springs eternal."

It was his father's favorite expression. Just like he often spoke of the day when he would see again. More than once he'd told Judd, Suzy, and their mother, "When I get to heaven, I'm going to spend the first hundred years looking at each of your faces."

During his lifetime, Judd's dad had tried a number of operations that it was hoped would fix his eyes. He'd gone blind at fourteen, during an attack of scarlet fever. That was unusual, even for the fifties when his father grew up. Scarlet fever by then had become a virtual relic. But not in his father's community in Communist Poland, where he grew up. He'd come to the U.S. in the seventies on a special student exchange and had stayed.

It was a well-known story in their town. His father had become a mathematician working out the complex geometries of rocket science, and a computer enthusiast. Even without his sight, he had excelled.

As Judd greeted his sister and father at the door, his father said, "Let's go to Walgate's for some ice cream. My treat."

"Yeah, right," Judd said. "Like he doesn't do this after every game."

"Think of it as a first," Mr. Lezerian said.

Suzy added, "You were great, Judd. I told Daddy about every move."

Pumpin' Premium

Hope is not just for people in bad circumstances. All of life revolves around hope. A boy calls up a girl to ask her to go out with him, and he does so with hope in his heart. A quarterback passes a ball to an end in hope of a catch and maybe a touchdown. A mother steps into her car and heads for the supermarket in hope that she'll be able to get all the food she needs for the family.

These are small hopes. They're important and we should never discount or disregard them. While we may have the single majestic hope of eternal life and salvation, and Christ's return, we must also live in the here and now. Day by day we need to maintain an attitude that life is worth living, that knowing Christ is a great gift, and that there is always reason to believe in the future. Such an attitude comes in the little things and through the little victories of life.

In the book of Proverbs, King Solomon says, "Hope deferred makes the heart sick, but desire fulfilled is a tree of life" (Proverbs 13:12). He meant that when we reach a point in life where we can no longer hope, we slip into despair and illness. Our hearts become "sick." But when we hope and then have that hope fulfilled, we sit under the shade of a tree of life. We live again. Life suddenly becomes a valued and joyous gift.

What are some of the little hopes that you find yourself thinking about? What expectations did you have today? Did you pray about them? Have you asked the Lord to get involved in even these aspects of your life?

If not, then start doing it now. God wants not only to be a part of everything, but to give you the desires of your heart as they conform to his desires.

Hit the Gas!

1. Name three small things you hoped for at different times today. Did any come to pass? Which ones? How did you feel about each? _____

_____

_____

2. Look at Ephesians 5:20. What is this thanks that we are to be giving all the time? How does it relate to our hopes? _____

_____

_____

_____

THURSDAY

Dad's Promotion

Judd drove and picked up their mother on the way. She was a lawyer, and though she normally made the games, she had a heavy caseload at the moment and wasn't able to attend. At the ice cream shop, they all ate banana splits and talked about Judd's possible "promotion."

"You know," Mr. Lezerian said, "if you get that three-point shot of yours perfected, nobody will be able to take that starting spot from you. No one else on the team has one."

"How do you know that, Dad?" Judd asked.

"I keep him informed," Suzy said.

"I can *feel* it, too," their father said. "I feel that little cone of air that swishes out when a ball drops through the hoop without touching the rim."

"Well, neither of mine did that tonight."

"But your three-pointers do. And you have another year."

That was Judd's dream. To play in the number-one left forward slot the whole of his senior year. Craig Morgan would graduate this year, and there was no one coming up among the freshmen or sophs who was close to Judd. So even if he didn't play much this year, there was a good chance he would next year.

As they finished their ice cream, Mr. Lezerian turned to his wife. "Well, should we tell them?"

"I guess so," their mother replied.

"What?" Suzy asked.

Judd just waited.

"I got a promotion at work," said Mr. Lezerian.

"Yes!" Judd cried.

"I knew he would do it!" Suzy answered.

"Well, it means we don't have to move," Mr. Lezerian added.

The problem had been hanging over all their heads. But now that it had come through, everyone was happy, especially Judd. A new school and new team would be especially tough. He liked it right where he was.

Pumpin' Premium

One thing about hope is that we all *have* hopes: our parents, our friends, our brothers and sisters. While we've concentrated on having hope ourselves, what about others? How can we participate in others' hopes, helping *them* to come to pass?

Years ago there was a circus clown named "Weary Willie the Hobo," created by Emmett Kelly. He could make a crowd laugh at his little capers with canes, balloons, fans, amateur juggling, and in numerous other ways. He was a jack of all trades.

One thing about Willie, though, was that he always ended up on the losing side. He rarely won. He blew his balloons too big and they burst in his face, making him cry. His cane slipped out from under him and he fell flat on his face. The crowd would laugh at all Weary Willy's problems. But they also identified with him. He never had any good luck, but he hung in there and kept on trying and trying. He had his dreams and went after them. It was that outlook that touched millions of onlookers as they laughed at and with Willie when things went wrong.

Why was his performance so powerful? Because we saw in him a little glimmer of ourselves and our families; in fact, of all humanity. We go up against towering odds and many times we lose. But sometimes we win—that's what keeps us in the game.

Similarly, we all need to look at one another as people of hope. We need to encourage those who have failed and lost their hope, reminding them that there are other dreams, other highways to the land of joy. Like it says in Hebrews, "Let us consider how to stimulate one another to love and good deeds . . . encouraging one another; and all the more, as you see the day drawing near" (Hebrews 10:24-25).

Who can you encourage to have new or renewed hope today?

Hit the Gas!

1. Take a look at the faces you see in the hallways at school. What do you see in their eyes? How does hope look in the eyes of someone who's really hoping? What does hopelessness look like?

_____

_____

_____

2. What Scripture might you share with someone who has lost hope or had his hopes dashed? Look at Hebrews 10:24-25. What does this Scripture offer us by way of stoking one another's hopes? _____

_____

_____

FRIDAY

Tragedy Strikes

As they all got into the car, Mr. Lezerian grabbed Judd by the shoulders and seemed to be peering at him from behind his dark glasses. He usually took a walking stick when he went places, but with the family, one of the kids or his mother would lead him. "I'm real proud of you, son. You did well tonight."

"Yeah; well, I just wish you could have seen it."

"So do I. Someday, though."

Judd got into the driver's seat and started the car. They turned onto the main drag leading out of town to the development where the Lezerians lived. It was a happy ride, full of cheer and talk about the future. Suzy asked plenty of questions about the new position, and Judd made his usual comments about the fact that his Dad could do anything.

No one heard the gunfire. There was just a sharp ping and the front passenger-side window was punctured. Then Mr. Lezerian slumped forward.

"Tret!" Mrs. Lezerian yelled.

"He's bleeding!" Suzy screamed.

Judd didn't wait for anyone to say what to do. He swung the car around and floored the accelerator toward town and the local hospital. Mrs. Lezerian crawled into the front seat and held her husband's head. She was crying and so was Suzy. Judd fought back an urge to scream and cry out, but he kept his presence of mind in order to get them to the emergency room.

Mr. Lezerian was unconscious when they rolled him into the ER.

Everyone sat out in the waiting room while Dr. Langston, a friend, drove to the hospital. Mr. Lezerian was taken into surgery.

At 11:14 p.m. Dr. Langston walked somberly out into the waiting room. There had been two other shootings that night. Apparently some kids—a local gang—had been sniping; no one had been caught yet.

Everyone stood as Dr. Langston came toward them. His eyes were brimming with tears. He said, "I'm so sorry, Nancy. I'm so sorry."

Pumpin' Premium

Sometimes our world is so full of tragedy and pain that it's hard to see the good for all the bad. Horrors like the above seem to happen every day. There is so much evil around us that giving in to despair and becoming a drug junkie, or dropping out and just "living for the day" can look like worthwhile options.

God doesn't spare Christians from tragedies. Christians are persecuted, hated, shot, rejected, banished. Being a Christian doesn't mean you could never get AIDS, even if you commit no sexual sins. Being a Christian doesn't guarantee you'll have a happy and wonderful life by the world's standards. Christian businesses fail. Christian students flunk tests and quit school. Christian sports figures lose games.

But over it all, God has written something that has greater power than any defeat, loss, or mistake: "Let not your heart be troubled; believe in God, believe also in Me. In My Father's house are many dwelling places; if it were not so, I would have told you; for I go to prepare a place for you. And if I go and prepare a place for you, I will come again, and receive you to Myself; that where I am, there you may be also" (John 14:1-3).

No matter how difficult things are now, God promises that there's something that will overshadow any pain we have to endure in this life.

Alexander Solzhenitsyn is a Russian writer who was imprisoned in the Soviet Union's death camps during the middle part of this century. At that time, anyone who spoke out against the Russian leaders was sent to Siberia. Solzhenitsyn writes of how he reached a point of complete hopelessness. Working twelve hours a day at hard labor, while being fed a starvation diet, he became ill. The doctors said it was over for him. One day, as he was shoveling sand under a searing sun, Solzhenitsyn stopped working. He stood there and waited for the guards to come and beat him. He resolved not to resist, but simply to die.

Then, as he waited, a fellow Christian prisoner walked toward him. With a cane, the friend etched a cross in the sand at Solzhenitsyn's feet. Strangely, the hope of life with Christ surged in the prisoner's heart. It was as if that hope gave him new strength and power. He went on working and eventually survived that terrible time.

Truly, hope is a source of strength and power to those who will let it burn inside them.

Hit the Gas!

1. What in this world gives you the greatest despair? What does the Bible say about that thing? Can you think of a verse or passage that relates to it? _____

_____

_____

2. Read 2 Corinthians 1:8-11. Paul tells about a time when he almost gave up hope. What did God do in response? How was Paul's hope kept alive? What does that say about how God works in us? _____

_____

_____

WEEKEND

Today Something Wonderful Happened

It was a tragedy the whole town was aware of by the next morning. The phone at the house rang constantly. Mrs. Lezerian wouldn't talk. Judd holed up in his room for the weekend and came out only to try to comfort his mother and sister. Relatives flew in from everywhere.

The whole basketball team came to the funeral on Tuesday.

Afterward, Coach Pellerend said to Judd in the hall, "You don't have to show up for the game tomorrow night, Judd. But I want you to know, it's dedicated to your Dad."

"I'm coming," Judd said. "Do I get to start?"

"Are you sure?"

"Yes. Will you let me start?"

"Okay."

Wednesday night, when his name was announced, along with the information that the game had been dedicated to his father, the people cheered and wept along with Judd and his family.

Judd played the best game of his life. The coach never took him out, and even Craig Morgan congratulated him at the end. He received the game ball and a special plaque. His family was interviewed for the TV news. The reporter asked Judd how it was that he'd played so well. Judd said, "It was for my dad. He was blind. But I know he has his eyesight back now that he's in heaven, and I feel like this might have been the first time he ever saw me play."

Later that month, the two young men responsible for the shootings were caught. It was a small consolation to the Lezerian family, but Judd continued playing basketball as he never had before in his life. Knowing his father might be watching made him give an effort he didn't know he had to give.

Pumpin' Premium

The first game of the World Series in October 1988 was a scorcher. The Oakland Athletics led in the ninth inning, with two outs, and it looked like the Los Angeles Dodgers would lose. Then the Dodgers' manager, Tommy LaSorda, sent in Kirk Gibson as a pinch hitter. Gibson had two bad legs. He could hardly run. He could hardly bat. Why LaSorda even called him up amazed almost everyone.

Soon the count was 3-2 and it looked hopeless.

And then Gibson gunned one into the bleachers. Home run. The game was over and the Dodgers won, 5-4. The whole stadium went wild.

You see things like that in sports rarely, just enough so that no game looks like it's over till it's over! In the same way, this world can look like Satan's playpen. Everywhere you turn, God and his people are getting their heads kicked. Abortion, homosexuality, greed, broken families—all of it just seems to get worse and worse.

But the Bible keeps telling us, "Jesus' day is coming. It's not over yet. Christ will come again and fix this mess, and nothing Satan can do will stop it!"

The Book of Revelation puts it succinctly: "Yes, I am coming quickly" (Revelation 22:20).

Well, it's been almost two thousand years since those words were written. But they are as true today as they were then. It could happen any moment. Jesus will come, and all the pains of this life will be forgotten. We will rejoice to see our moms and dads and granddads and grandmoms together forever. Paul will be there. And Peter, Thomas, Andrew, King David, Abraham, Ruth, Sarah, Rebekah. And of course, *Jesus!*

I wonder who I'll talk to first. What about you?

Hit the Gas!

1. Think about what you've learned in the above section about hope. How often does the Bible offer us hope while we're still in this world? How often after we're beyond it? Which is the more important? Why? _____

_____

_____

2. Read Revelation 19:11-16. What kind of thoughts and hopes does this passage stir in you? Do you look forward to that moment? Why, or why not? _____

_____

_____

Week Four

Never Give Up!

MONDAY

No Way Out

Shelly Ferrarra blinked repeatedly. The snow seemed right in her eyes, even though the windshield wipers batted the flakes away with a mesmerizing shoosh, shoosh. "Brian, please be careful. This is a back road."

"I know," her boyfriend Brian Sipple answered. "Isn't it great?"

"Just be careful."

"I am. I'm driving as slow as my mom would."

Brian turned his eyes forward and grinned. Shelly saw the smile and shuddered. *If he wasn't so cute, the guy would be a complete ditz*, she thought.

They had been surprised by the snowstorm. They'd gone skiing with the youth group in the Pennsylvania mountains, staying at Brian's uncle's cabin far back in the woods. No one had been listening to the radio or TV, they were all so intent on skiing. The youth pastor and his wife had cleared out less than an hour before, getting assurances from Shelly that they'd be leaving in minutes. But one thing led to another, with little things to clean up here and there. She was not going to let Brian leave the place a mess as they had the previous year.

Shelly listened to the whoosh of the snow around the car. It was a fearsome storm, with the wind rising and splattering the snow in great swishes and yaws across the car and the windshield.

"Watch it up here, Brian. It's curvy."

"I know. I've been here more often that you have."

"You don't have to get nasty about it."

73

"Shelley! Just be quiet and let me drive, okay?"

Shelley didn't enjoy being a nag. She'd seen enough of that in her mother. But Brian was definitely driving too fast.

"Brian, please!"

"Oh, no!"

There was a sharp rattle of stones and wood under the engine and the floorboards. Then the car crunched to a stop in front of a tree. The windshield wipers went on swishing. The head lamps shone into the forest, illuminating the snowfall in an eerie glow. Everything else was silent.

"I'll check it out," he said.

Shelley didn't respond. She glumly thought of having to get out of the warm car, dig out, and then push. She envisioned snow and mud all over her jeans and new ski jacket. And the cold; it was *so* cold. Why did this have to happen?

Pumpin' Premium

Nearly every day, each of us will face problems that try our patience. The wintry accident described here is the beginning of something difficult. It's one of those situations that present few options: You're in it and have to tough it out to the end.

What resources do you tap into when you find yourself in a real life or death trial? How do you summon courage or determination or strength? Where does it come from?

In the 1800s, William Wilberforce was a member of Parliament and one of the first British politicians to oppose slavery in England. He was also a committed Christian. As he voiced his dissent over the English policy toward slavery, the same issue had begun to sizzle in the U.S. It would eventually lead to the Civil War.

But Wilberforce wanted a peaceful solution. As he pressed his case, he was abused in the press, accused of being a wife-beater, smeared as immoral. None of these accusations was true, but it was a media and personal battle that would last twenty years. On his deathbed, the evangelist John Wesley, whose preaching had turned the English world upside down, wrote a letter of encouragement to Wilberforce. In it, Wesley said, "Unless God has raised you up for this very thing, you will be worn out by the opposition of men and devils; but if God be for you, who can be against you? Are all of them together stronger than God? Be not weary in well-doing."

Wilberforce never wavered, and eventually led Britain to a peaceful freeing of all slaves in its realm.

Another powerful word comes from Paul: "Be steadfast, immovable, always abounding in the work of the Lord, knowing that your toil is not in vain in the Lord" (1 Corinthians 15:58).

This week we'll be looking at the all-important issue of endurance and perseverance—staying in the battle to the end. Think about the words of John Wesley and Paul as you proceed. God is with those who are his. If he is for us, who can be against us?

Hit the Gas!

1. How big is God? How great is he? Make some comparisons between him and the biggest problem you have at the moment. _____

_____

_____

2. Meditate on 1 Corinthians 15:58. What does this verse say to you about hanging in there when things are tough? _____

_____

_____

TUESDAY

Really Stuck

"We're dead in the water," Brian informed Shelley after spinning the wheels in both directions. He couldn't even get it to rock. "I think we're caught on some big rocks."

"Now what do we do?"

"Radar central control?"

"Don't joke about this, Brian. This is serious."

"Will you quit being my mother for one minute?"

Shelley sulked and stared into the night. It was past ten o'clock. No one would miss them till morning, probably. It was a six-hour drive. The youth pastor had promised to give them a call at 8 A.M. But that was the earliest anyone would know anything.

The cabin didn't even have a phone; it was disconnected for the winter. And it was another mile or so to the main road. If the storm would just end, they could probably walk to the highway and hitchhike to a service station.

"Should we leave on the lights like this, Brian?" Shelley called out as she opened the window. Snow blew in briskly, pecking her face and chilling her neck. She rolled up the window, leaving it open an inch.

"I'm looking for a flashlight."

Shelly waited until Brian came around and jumped back inside. "Man, it's cold," he said, rubbing his hands together. "I packed my ski mittens and hat."

"I know. I didn't expect this, either. What should we do?"

"Make out?"

"Brian!"

76

"Okay." He switched off the lights and then the engine. "We could get carbon monoxide poisoning if we leave it running. So we can't leave the heat on. I think we should get all our stuff out of the trunk and bed down."

" 'Bed down'?"

"No use walking in the storm. We'll just get lost. There's at least eight inches now and we could lose the road real easy."

"Yeah, I guess I agree."

"So, you want the back seat or the front?"

"I'll take the front. I'm smaller."

"Thanks. Though if you want to cuddle up together in the back, I'd . . ."

"I'll pass on that for the moment, Brian."

"Thanks a lot."

Pumpin' Premium

God wants us to persevere in the Christian life. But persevering doesn't always mean "doing" something. In a trying situation, action isn't always what is called for. Sometimes we need to relax, rest, get a good night's sleep. Waiting out the storm is a wise thing to do in the situation that Shelly and Brian face. They could do nothing to change their circumstances, and pressing out into the storm would have been foolhardy.

What is a comparable situation in the Christian life? One might be our need for spiritual thought and prayer before tackling a tough job. Spending time in the Word and praying often lead to practical insights that make a job easier. As one of my professors used to say, "Work smarter, not harder."

That's a key to persevering in the Christian life. Work smarter, not harder. For example, take Bible reading in small bites. They add up. Reading four chapters a day will get you through the whole Bible in a year. That's much easier than marathoning on

Sunday or at 5 A.M. on Monday, intending to make it through a whole book the size of Genesis or Isaiah.

Another idea is just as simple: Walk, don't run. Walter Elliott wrote in *The Spiritual Life*, "Perseverance is not a long race; it is many short races one after another." Perhaps I can modify it a bit: "Perseverance is a long walk with many stops, starts, restarts, and occasional jogs and sprints along the way."

Most of us can't jog without getting winded some distance from the starting line. But many of us can walk for miles. That's perseverance: plodding, walking, just taking one step after another. In the spiritual life that means taking growth in small chunks and bites. Read a few Bible verses a night, every night. Pray each day for three minutes at bedtime. Try to share the gospel at least once a week. Go to church for the main service, then try to add others—like the Sunday evening service, or midweek youth group. Just keep chugging along.

Abraham Lincoln was once asked how he intended to win the Civil War.

"Just keep pegging and pegging away," was Lincoln's reply. That's the Christian life. That's perseverance.

Hit the Gas!

1. What aspects of Christian living do you find the easiest? The hardest? What can you do to make the harder parts easier, and take them in smaller bites? _____

_____

_____

2. Read Paul's prescription for perseverance in 2 Corinthians 12:1-10. What does this passage reveal about God's work in us to help us persevere? _____

_____

_____

WEDNESDAY

Hunger

Dawn came with the snow still swirling. The car was cold, but buried in their weekend clothes, pajamas, and a blanket and comforter that each had brought, they had remained warm. Shelley woke up first. It was about 7 A.M. She lay still, listening to the snow. The continuing snow prevented the morning from brightening much. The cloud cover was thick still; she could see that out the window, even though it was snow-dusted and icy with frost.

"Brian?"

Shelley waited a full minute before speaking again. "Brian?"

"Hmmmmm?"

"Are you awake?"

"Not yet."

"Well, better get yourself in gear. We've got to get out of here."

She heard him roll over and then begin untangling himself from the mound of clothes covering him. A moment later he peeked over the edge of the back seat. "You okay?"

She smiled, then noticed that her mouth tasted like stale hot chocolate. "I'm hungry."

"So am I. Do we have anything?"

Shelley nodded. "I have a candy bar and some Crackerjacks. And there was the stuff left over that we didn't throw away. Some hamburger. Frozen, I'm sure."

"I'll eat anything. Look, I'll make a fire."

"With what?"

Brian looked around. "The cigarette lighter, of course."

Pumpin' Premium

Food is something few of us ever get tired of. When you're hungry, nothing satisfies like food.

That was a heavy insight, wasn't it?

Seriously, comparing endurance and Christian living to hunger is a good analogy. Peter told his readers, "Like newborn babes, long for the pure milk of the word, that by it you may grow in respect to salvation" (1 Peter 2:2). Yesterday we looked at how we need to learn to take spiritual living in small bites and chunks. Peter's words make us think about taking it in slurps and gulps. But Peter's idea is that we "long for" the Word as a baby desires milk.

Ever see a baby with a milk bottle—when he's really hungry? Don't try to rip that bottle out of his hands, unless you're wearing earmuffs! Babies want what they want when they want it.

Brian and Shelly had to prepare themselves for a long walk through deep drifts and numbing cold. Eating something was wise. Any coach, military officer, or leader knows the need to keep his troops fed and strong. Hungry people are unhappy, weak, hurting, and miserable.

To persevere as a Christian—keep in the race till the end—we must cultivate the habit of feeding on spiritual things so that it becomes part of the pattern of our lives. Perseverance doesn't happen by dropping out or getting bloated once a year on spiritual ice cream. It happens by eating right and eating regularly. We need a healthy balance of veggies, meat, and drink. In the spiritual realm, we might compare those foods to doing good, giving, and obeying; or witnessing, planting seeds, and waiting; or praying, giving thanks, and praising. Everything must be kept in an invigorating balance.

A man we all know of is a powerful portrait of perseverance. Some have catalogued the main events of his life like this:

At seven, his family was forced out of their home.

At nine, his mother died.

At 22, he lost a job as a clerk. He longed to attend law school, but didn't have enough education to be admitted.

At 23, he indebted himself to go into business. At 26, his partner died, leaving him a debt that would cost him years to pay off.

At 28, he asked a girl he'd courted for four years to marry him. She refused.

At 37, after three tries, he was elected to Congress. Two years later, he lost his re-election bid and returned to private life.

At 45, he lost a race for U.S. senator.

At 49, he again lost a senatorial election.

At 51, he was elected President of the United States.

Have you figured out who this man was? Abraham Lincoln. At almost any point before winning the presidency, Lincoln might have been considered a colossal failure. But he persevered, and in the end he became the man whom many consider the greatest President we have ever had.

He was a man who persevered against terrible odds. And won.

Hit the Gas!

1. Read Psalm 3. Here David laments a terrible situation wherein he has found himself surrounded by enemies. But he also has found hope and heart . . . in what? In whom? How did his faith in God help him to persevere? _____

_____

2. Who is one person you'd consider a model of perseverance? What is it about that person that you think enables him or her to stay in the race when others might quit? _____

_____

THURSDAY

Go Forward or Die!

A fire was burning under the boughs of an evergreen next to the car. Brian poked his head in the door. "Breakfast can be made now."

"Oh, *I* have to make it?"

"I made the fire, you make the vittles."

Shelley rigged up a little cooking tin with some aluminum foil they had in the trunk. The meat was cooked in less than twenty minutes, and they both enjoyed a large portion of meat loaf, followed by two Clark Bars for dessert.

"I guess now we have to walk," Brian said.

"Shouldn't you try the car?"

"Where would we go? I bet it snowed over two feet."

Shelley peered up the road. "Yeah. How far is it to the main road?"

"It's over a mile from the road to the cabin. We probably came half that distance last night. Maybe a half-mile. Then all we do is hitch."

"Sounds good to me."

Dressed in their ski outfits, they made it to the road after a two-hour hike. But it wasn't even a state highway. The road wasn't plowed. Brian and Shelley looked in both directions; there were no plows, no sounds of cars or trucks, nothing in either direction as far as they could see. Neither of them had expected anything like this.

Hiking through the drifts had been exhausting. The snow was still falling, too.

"*Now* what do we do?" Brian asked. His voice was low. Shelley knew it was his way of concealing his fear.

"Keep walking?"

"It'll be noon in an hour, Shell. And how far is it to town—six miles or so? We've got to go back."

"Go back and do what?"

"I don't know."

"I say let's head for town. At least there we can call our parents."

"It'll be tough. We're pushing through more than two feet of snow now. And I'm freezing."

"We can't go back, Brian. Our only hope is to keep going forward."

"All right. You win."

Pumpin' Premium

Aesop told one of his famous fables about a crow. The bird was half-dead with thirst when it happened upon a pitcher containing only a little water. Bending down, he found he could not reach the water for the tight neck of the pitcher. After many tries, he gave up in despair. He had reached his limit. He would die.

But then he spied something and an idea popped into his head. It was a pebble. He dropped it into the pitcher and the water rose slightly. Eagerly, happily, he dropped in more pebbles until the water level was high enough for him to drink all he wanted. Aesop's moral is: "Little by little does the trick."

Perseverance in the Christian life—taking it a step at a time—is a key to spiritual survival. I can't emphasize that point enough. Many Christians start off on fire and end up as cinders. They go up like a rocket, and down like a rock. Jesus even told a parable about the need for perseverance—the parable of the four soils. Two kinds of soil failed to persevere. The seed sprouted in the rocky soil, but when the sun came up, the young plants withered, because the seed had no root. The seed in the weedy soil sprang up, but because it was surrounded by weeds and briars, it eventually was choked out.

Jesus makes the application that some people who hear the Word of God and appear to believe do not follow through. When trials come and it becomes hard to be a Christian, they give up. Or, the believer's desire for money and pleasure eventually chokes out his faith.

It can happen to any of us. Jesus is giving a warning. We need to "make sure of our calling," as Peter said (2 Peter 1:10). God is utterly serious about us and our need to keep on keeping on. In one sense, our salvation is secure in Christ. "Once saved, always saved," is an expression that is true as far as it goes. But it doesn't go far enough. It should say, "The one saved will continue to be saved by persevering in his salvation."

There's no way around it. True believers endure. They stick with it. They don't give up.

Hit the Gas!

1. Read James 1:12-16 . What does this passage reveal about perseverance? How can you apply it to a trial you're going through right now? _____

_____

_____

2. Is perseverance only useful when we go through trials? What about the good times, the easy times? How does perseverance work then? _____

_____

_____

FRIDAY

All Hope Gone

"Let's just rest for a while, Shelley. You know, sit? Have you heard of sitting?"

"That's how people freeze to death. It'll be dark in an hour. We have to make it."

"Don't forget whose idea this was."

Shelley slogged on. In a moment, Brian caught up. "I'm sorry, Shell. But this is getting to me."

"We have to keep going, Brian. There's no stopping now!" She was close to tears, more afraid than she'd ever been in her life, and frozen through. The blinding snow continued; it was like no storm she'd ever seen. How could it have happened this weekend? Why hadn't it come after she was home in bed, under six comforters?

For the most part, Brian was content to keep his thoughts to himself. He had begun talking again, after nearly an hour, when suddenly he stumbled, fell face forward, and a paralyzing crack broke the winter silence.

Shelley grabbed his arm and helped him up.

"I smashed my knee. A pothole."

"Is it bad?"

They stumbled a moment in the snow. "Just let me rest," he said.

She held him and they both settled down in a heap. After a kiss and a few reassuring words, Shelley said, "Do you think you can walk?"

"I don't know."

"We have to, Brian. We have to."

"I don't know if I can, Shelley. I'm not a miracle worker."

There was a fearful silence. Then Shelley said, "Let me help you over to the side of the road."

"Then what?"

"We'll build an igloo or something."

"An igloo?"

"If you can't walk, we have to get some warmth. The best way is under the snow in a little enclosed area. I've read about it. Don't look at me like that. The sun is going down, I can't even see the lights of town, and we can't just sit here. We'll break off some evergreen boughs and make a little shelter."

"Oh, you mean this time we *do* get to sleep in one another's arms?"

Shelley laughed. "Yes, dear one. Your dream is coming true."

"Maybe we should pray then?"

"I've been praying every inch of this journey."

"Okay, but let's pray together." They stopped, bowed their heads, and prayed. Then Shelley helped Brian struggle off to the side of the road. Down a small incline, she found a cluster of evergreens. With Brian standing on one leg to do his part, they broke off branches and built a little lean-to in the deep snow.

When they finally crawled inside, the wind was picking up. But it swirled around them, and they found some warmth and security in their shelter. After getting Brian settled, Shelley sat down next to him. "I wish we had a cigarette lighter."

"'I wish we had some food," Brian said.

"Yeah. About six Big Macs."

Pumpin' Premium

There's no easy way to "hang tough," "make a comeback," or stick with a difficult situation "to the bitter end." It takes time, effort, and sometimes tears. The Christian life is not a hundred-yard dash. It's not even a marathon. It's a lifelong walk that includes breezy summer days, cool fall rain, harsh winter blows, and wet spring thaws. There are deserts, mountains, valleys, and long, long stretches of unexciting road. There's no way to make it all fun and happiness. There will be highs, lows, great joy, and great despair. Anyone who feels deeply and then becomes a Christian will feel even *more* deeply—and he will feel both the good and the bad with greater intensity.

I'm not trying to overwhelm you. But we need to be realistic. Christian living is *real life!* And it has all the grubbiness and scrubbiness of mud-caked shoes and stained dress shirts. There will be times when you want to give up, when you just wish the Lord would come and take you away. There will also be times when life and faith are so beautiful, you can't contain it; you just have to shout some praises!

In motion terminology, perseverance calls for running, walking, slogging, plodding, sprinting, staggering, stumbling, shambling, ambling, and helter-skelter go-for-the-gold galloping. There are no set formulas, no drawn-in-cement diagrams. It's just a matter of hanging in there with Jesus to the very end.

Years ago there was an article in *Reader's Digest* about a man named Jim Brunotte. Jim runs a ranch for handicapped people. His goal is to teach them to overcome by faith, determination, and hard work. He has only one arm and one eye. Both of his legs are cut off at the knees. Yet he is a man who perseveres. In 1979, President Jimmy Carter awarded him the "Handicapped American of the Year" plaque, our highest national honor for those among us who must struggle harder in life due to physical limitations. Jim is a naturally upbeat, confident person who always gives his all. He was asked if there weren't times, though, when his positive outlook really isn't just a legend he has to maintain. Jim responded with a huge grin, "You've got an option. Either you stand by the roadside and watch the world go by, or you get in there and fight" (*Reader's Digest*, August 1979).

That's the choice for all of us.

Hit the Gas!

1. Read 2 Timothy 2:3-6. What do Paul's analogies say about the nature of the Christian life? How do his words relate to *your* situation in life? How would you classify yourself—as a soldier, athlete, or farmer? Why? _____

_____

_____

2. Have you ever felt as if you had to fight for your Christian life? When? What happened? How did you come out in the end?

_____

_____

_____

WEEKEND

Do or Die

Another dawn came with both of them cold, sneezing, and stiff. Brian still couldn't walk. Shelley helped him up to the road and then they prayed, trying to decide what to do.

"A plow has to come through sometime," Brian said. The weather had given way to tiny, icy flakes of snow, not the pounding storm of the past two days.

"Yes, but we can't sit here, either. We'll get cold, then sleepy, and the next thing you know, we're frozen solid."

"You read that too?"

"Yeah."

Brian looked down the road. "Well, m'lady, give me your shoulder and I'll let you lead me to glory."

Staggering off together, they pushed through mounds of snow in pockets and drifts across the road. They had to find a way around many of the drifts; some were as deep as seven feet.

Brian said his leg was feeling better, but Shelley sensed he was just trying to sound upbeat.

As the morning wore on, the situation was beginning to take the fight out of Shelley. By noon she was so hungry and weak that she felt content just to sit most of the time, occasionally making a few feeble steps; she no longer cared whether she lived or died. Brian kept slapping her and shouting at her to keep on. But she was spent.

"You can't give up now!" Brian yelled.

Shelley didn't answer. Instead, she sat down in a drift and closed her eyes. "Let me rest a little," she murmured, ". . . just rest."

"No!" Brian screamed. "Wake up." He gripped her chin and pressed. "Get up, Shelley! Get up!"

Shelley lay back again, letting the touch of snow on her face caress her into a strange oblivious state. But in the back of her mind she heard something, something swishing, roaring, crying. For a moment, she thought she must be dead.

And then she heard Brian cry, "A plow! The plows are coming!"

Pumpin' Premium

One of the greatest things about knowing Jesus is that Christian faith is not all work and service. There's time for relief, relaxation, and fun, too. God is not without humor. He wants us to enjoy life. He doesn't want us to see the Christian walk as a grind.

So he provides moments of release and hope for each of us. Frequently, we get a word of encouragement, a pat on the back, an award. And at the end of an often grueling walk, we see the plows—and our hope and joy are rekindled.

Don't think of Christianity as either all fun and games or all homework and hard work. No, it's life. It includes everything—the laughs, the cries, the cheers, the raspy whimpers, the pained prayers at midnight.

I think of the story of Dave Dravecky, major league baseball pitcher for the San Francisco Giants. Diagnosed with cancer in his pitching arm, Dave nearly gave up baseball. But a valiant, stirring comeback brought him back to the majors. Over 55,000 fans saw him pitch his comeback game against the Cincinnati Reds on August 10, 1989. It seemed like everyone on earth was rooting for him, and Dave didn't disappoint. He pitched a winning game—after losing nearly half of the major muscle in his pitching arm to cancer. Until the top of the eighth inning, in fact, Dave pitched a shutout. He received over fourteen standing ovations that day.

Some said his was one of the most dramatic comebacks in base-ball history.

The next game Dave pitched, though, was a disaster. His weakened arm snapped and broke. He was out of baseball for good. Today, Dave is asked whether all the pain and agony was worth the struggle. He says, "I leave baseball with a great sense of satisfaction. When I think back on my career, I do so with a big, fat smile on my face. How could I feel anything else?

"Every year in America hundreds of thousands of kids go out to play Little League, and every year each of them dreams of playing in the major leagues. The odds are so slim. It's as if you had a huge stadium jammed full of kids, each wearing a uniform and a glove, and just one out of all those thousands got picked to come down onto the field and play with the big boys.

"I was that kid. I got to play with the big boys.

"And even more: I got the chance to come back."[1]

Dravecky's faith and perseverance paid off in baseball, and I'm sure they will be his greatest triumph as a Christian, too.

Persevering as a Christian isn't easy. And yet at the same time, it's not impossible. Because God is on our side. And we can be confident that he'll bring us through. Like Paul said, "I am con-fident of this very thing, that He who began a good work in you will perfect it until the day of Christ Jesus" (Philippians 1:6).

So hang in there. Keep on keeping on. The end is in sight. Jesus is coming.

Hit the Gas!

1. Read Paul's encouraging words to his disciple Timothy in 2 Timothy 1:3-7. Remember that Timothy was "on the skids" at that point in his spiritual life. How do you think Paul's words might have helped him? _____

_____

_____

2. What is your greatest fear as a Christian? Is it that you won't stay with your Christian walk to the end? Then why not commit your life again to the Lord, who promises to help you make good on your commitment? _____

_____

_____

Note:

1. Dave Dravecky with Tim Stafford, *Comeback* (Grand Rapids: Zondervan; and San Francisco: Harper & Row, 1990), p. 249.

Week Five

How to Get More Out of Life by Giving More to Life

MONDAY

Report on Giving

This report was found in the angelic archives of Gabriel, well-known angelic messenger in the Bible. In it, he reports to Michael, his superior, about his discoveries concerning giving by humans for the sake of God's kingdom. Here he investigates the results of the giving of the widow who gave two mites or "lepta"—a small coin—to the Temple treasury.

MEMO

TO: Michael, Archangel

FROM: Gabriel

RE: A study of divine accounting procedures, specifically those relating to the giving of a particular widow (as recorded in Mark 12:41-44), and one of the others participating in the same event, Zechariah, purported to have been a rich man (by human standards).

DATE: Last Days, June 12.

The accounting records are, as you indicated, superb. I had not realized they were so exact—though I should have expected this. I arrived at the recording chamber early. Daniel was courteous and efficient, as you said he would be. He took me directly to the recording angel for a look at the accounts on the widow.

But first he showed me some records for gifts given on that same Monday on which the widow gave her two mites. The ledger went as follows:

NAME	GIFT
Zechariah	1 talent (silver), 14 drachma, 6 lepta
Mallagran	23 drachma
Eli	4 minas, 22 drachma, 26 lepta
Mariel	12 drachma, 4 lepta
Matthel	2 minas, 6 drachma
The widow	2 lepta[1]

There was a break in the accounts at this point, because of Jesus' comments about the value of what the widow was putting in. He said, "Truly I say to you, this poor widow put in more than all the contributors to the treasury; for they all put in out of their surplus, but she, out of her poverty, put in all she owned, all she had to live on." It was a sound enough statement, but Satan has argued, through his lawyer, Zob, that the two mites (or lepta) that the widow put in hardly amounted to anything and could not possibly have counted as much as the others. The Lord has told Satan to wait till the end for the final accounting on that issue. I'm sure Jesus' words will be vindicated.

But also, because of the commotion around the widow, Satan said that three of his disciples in the line were overlooked. However, I found the records quite exact. Those three were:

Malchi	3 minas, 22 drachma, 2 lepta
Abel	16 drachma, 2 lepta
Canel	1 mina, 12 drachma, 2 lepta

Zob also argued that each of these three put in two lepta, the same as the widow, and that Jesus should have given them similar recognition. But this was clearly a case of devilogic and missing the point, and was thrown out of the Throne Room.

Pumpin' Premium

Giving of your wealth to the Lord was an important feature of spiritual life in Jesus' day, and it remains the same today. How we give—of our money, time, talents, and possessions—is a direct reflection of how much we love the Lord.

What was the basic difference between the widow and the others? We can see several comparisons:

The Widow	The Rich Men
Poor	Rich
Old	All ages
Two mites	Varying amounts
Gave all she had	Gave out of their surplus

That last distinction is the important one. What had the rich people been doing? They'd been giving, all right—far more than the widow's two mites. In fact, a mite at that time was less in value than a penny today. How is it that a person who gives two cents can be giving more than one who gives a hundred or five hundred or a thousand dollars?

We can say that God is seeing the attitude of the heart. But in practical terms, while the widow gave gloriously, just how far could those two mites go?

We'll find out in this week's study.

At the same time, ask yourself this question: What was it about the widow's gift that Jesus most respected?

There's a story of how Alexander the Great, who lived in the fourth century B.C. and conquered much of the known world for Greece and Macedonia, passed by a beggar who cried out for alms. Alexander pitched him several gold coins. One of Alexander's commanders protested, saying, "Sir, copper coins would have adequately met the beggar's needs. Why give gold?"

Alexander replied, "Yes, copper would have met his needs, but gold suits a conqueror's giving."

Alexander, even in his paganism, recognized the chief truth about giving: We should give in accordance with our wealth, not just in accordance with what may be needed. The poor widow gained more in the eyes of heaven than any of those rich men because she gave far beyond her means, presumably out of love and devotion to God.

Hit the Gas!

1. Read the story in Mark 12:41-44. What principles emerge from this text? How do you think others might react to Jesus' words, especially the rich people who gave so much? _____

_____

_____

2. What is your own policy or outlook on giving? Do you give—of your time, talents, and treasure—to serve the Lord? What are your motives? Have you seen any results in your life stemming from those actions? _____

_____

_____

TUESDAY

Where It All Went

The more interesting scenario is that of the *results* of the widow's two donated coins. What came of the money she gave? From a purely quantitative point of view, her gift was far less significant than any of the others. In fact, it was only enough to buy two minutes'-worth of a scribe's work. But as we know, the Lord doesn't work on the basis of economics. His kingdom is spiritually based. I pursued the matter and discovered the following:

The widow's gift was credited against the work of a certain scribe (Ezekijah) in their copy room. The Lord used the two lepta to pay for the scribe's time copying a portion of the prophet Isaiah's writings from a worn scroll to a new one. To be exact, the money was accounted as paying for the scribe's work from 2:46 to 2:48 in the afternoon on June 13 of that year. In that time slot, he copied from the old scroll the passage we know as Isaiah 53, verses four through six. Those verses read, "Surely our griefs He Himself bore, and our sorrows He carried; yet we ourselves esteem Him stricken, smitten of God, and afflicted. But He was pierced through for our transgressions, He was crushed for our iniquities; the chastening for our well-being fell upon Him, and by His scourging we are healed. All of us like sheep have gone astray, each of us has turned to his own way; but the Lord has caused the iniquity of us all to fall on Him."

(The Temple, of course, records the widow's lepta as going into a fund to replace the gold on some ceilings, and the actual pieces were used in an illegal money-changing transaction that ended up in the hands of a Pharisee—Zepheli. But that has little to do with the divine accounting, as we know. God doesn't work as men work.)

But back to the scroll. This new scroll remained in the Temple for several years. Many of the apostles read from this portion and used it to prove Jesus was the Messiah. More than four thousand lost souls (4,322, by angelic reckoning) were reclaimed during this period. The Apostle Paul himself used the passage frequently. He had a direct effect on some 36,755 people (up until his beheading). Only omniscience can bring all these things together statistically, of course.

But let me explain this a little more thoroughly.

Pumpin' Premium

In the above report, Gabriel discovers something amazing and dramatic. (We don't know if this is how things really work in heaven, but considering God's power and wisdom, it seems reasonable that he *might* work this way.)

At any rate, Gabriel follows the path of the widow's mites through history. He begins to see how many people were affected by her gift. Of course, our account here is fiction, but Scripture teaches that God can and will "supply all your needs according to His riches in glory in Christ Jesus" (Philippians 4:19). Certainly that includes our eternal and spiritual needs.

Have you ever wondered how the money you give for God's work is used? Have you ever thought that your gift of a quarter, or a dollar, or a few dollars couldn't go very far when you look at prices today? A dollar will barely buy a candy bar, let alone something of great value—like a translation of the Bible or someone's air fare to a faraway land.

But this kind of thinking discounts what God really *is* able to do with our gifts. Remember the Bible story of the boy who went to hear Jesus? He took his lunch—two pieces of smoked fish and five small bits of bread. Andrew befriended the boy, and when

Jesus asked the disciples what food they had, Andrew volunteered the boy's lunch. (Presumably he did this with the boy's approval; this wasn't a railroad job!) Jesus took that tiny portion of food and multiplied it so that it fed 5,000 people. According to the Hebrew way of counting, though, that 5,000 number only included the *men*. With women and children, that figure could have jumped to twelve or fifteen thousand.

But even if it was 5,000, that's quite a miracle. Everyone recognized it as a stupendous work. In a day and age when food was scarce, a person who could multiply loaves and fishes like that was truly a wonder worker.

In the same way, God takes our smallest offerings and multiplies them for good in ways we can't see—just as my fictional account shows being done with the widow's mites. It's all a matter of the giver's heart. If your heart is right, God can do literally anything. And one day we'll all *see* what he's done!

Hit the Gas!

1. Read the story of the loaves and fishes. It's in all four gospels, but the strongest version is in John 6:1-21. Again, what does this story say about God's ability to make the most out of our gifts? _____

_____

_____

2. Think about your own giving. When you give some of your money or time, how do you feel about it? What aspects of giving make you feel happy, as if you have pleased God? What aspects don't? _____

_____

_____

WEDNESDAY

Spreading the News

In my continuing investigation, I found that Peter read from Isaiah 53 several times during that year, in answer to objections from Pharisees. In one of those readings, a young man named David ben Matthew was listening. He was a learned Jew, though young, and believed Jesus had not been the Messiah.

However, upon hearing Peter's exposition of the words in Isaiah 53—verse six to be precise; it says man's iniquities were laid on Christ—this man's heart was pricked. The Spirit spoke to him, and he became a believer at that moment.

Now what does this have to do with the widow?

First, it was her lepta that paid for those words to be written, as I've already said.

But second, the Lord's accounting involves a rather important system of "royalties." That is, any effect that comes from something someone gave to be used for the faith is as much a part of the deed as the gift itself. Thus, any future good brought about by that particular passage in Isaiah goes to the widow's account (and to the account of anyone else who was involved; for example, I found out that the widow herself had been given one lepta by an old man of faith, so he profits, too).

Anyway, the fact is that every time those verses were read by Peter or anyone else, whatever kingdom effects resulted were credited to the widow's account! That means that the widow will ultimately be rewarded not only for the two lepta given in faith, but for everything that proceeded from that gift.

Frankly, Michael, I found myself wishing I were that widow! But there's more . . .

Pumpin' Premium

There's a story I've read of the poverty that struck London after World War II. Many people went without luxuries or even the basic necessities for years. On one occasion, an American GI passed along a street and saw a little English boy standing in front of a bakery shop, his nose pressed against the window. He watched the baker knead the dough and produce a fresh batch of doughnuts.

The soldier scrutinized the scene a moment, then walked over. "Son," he said, "Would you like some of those?"

The boy nodded his head. "Oh, yes, I sure would."

The soldier went inside and a moment later came out with a dozen doughnuts. He pressed the sack of doughnuts into the boy's hands. "Here you are!" he said.

The soldier smiled, then began to walk away. But the boy grabbed his coat and stopped him. He said, "Mister, are you God?"

That child wasn't joking. But there's a truth there. We are never more like God than when we give gladly, sacrificially, offering more than what was needed.

2 Corinthians 9:7 says, "God loves a cheerful giver."

If the widow had known all that her two mites would accomplish, don't you think she would have given even more cheerfully? That's undoubtedly the reason that story was included in the Bible. God wants us to know how much he enjoys and applauds cheerful, sacrificial giving. You may feel your gifts are small or even useless. But that's human thinking. God looks at it differently.

Hit the Gas!

1. Read 2 Corinthians 9:6-8. How does this passage give us insight into God's plan for our giving? What principles can you apply in your life this week? _____

_____

_____

2. Are you a cheerful giver? How can you give more cheerfully—even *hilariously*—as the original word meant? _____

_____

_____

THURSDAY

It Keeps Getting Bigger!

Beyond all that I've mentioned is the fact that this scroll went on to become the standard on which many of the later scrolls were based. We record that 433,622,565 people have been influenced by that text from that day to the present hour, but those figures change every moment.

By way of angel-interest stories, let me relate to you the following facts. You will recall an episode in which one of our number instructed Philip to walk down to a road leading toward Gaza. (You can find this story in Acts 8:26-40; how I wish Luke had been able to fit more in about it.)

Anyway, there Philip met an Ethiopian, a eunuch; he was an official of the high court of Candace, queen of the Ethiopians. This man was reading from a text of Isaiah, and Philip asked him if he understood it. He didn't. Then Philip explained the text, turned the man to Jesus, and baptized him.

What text was the Ethiopian reading? The one the widow's lepta were used to copy! I'm still investigating how the Master engineered this one. But for now I'll file it under "Unsearchable Wisdom."

So this eunuch went back to his kingdom a Christian. He spoke to Candace of his newfound faith, led several in her court to Christ, and eventually went on to become a powerful evangelist in that land. To this day, the church he began there lives on.

And all this—all those souls, all that good, everything that happened to advance the kingdom of the Lord—will go to the widow's account. She'll be one of the richest folks in heaven—no doubt about it! That is, if there could be such comparisons in heaven (which there can't).

Pumpin' Premium

Imagine that widow's amazement were she to learn these things in heaven! She might have wished she had given more. But how could she? Jesus said she had given all she had.

And that was the point.

I have read that there are seven ways of giving. They are:

1. *The careless way.* Just giving to a cause because the speaker lifts your emotions, even though his cause may be without real merit.

2. *The impulsive way.* Giving irregularly, especially when your emotions or desire to show love are touched.

3. *The lazy way.* To give by promoting special projects at church, such as bake sales, garage sales, fairs, and so on.

4. *The self-denying way.* Refusing luxuries at home and giving the money saved to worthy causes as the Lord directs.

5. *The systematic way.* Saving regularly and giving at appropriate times what you have saved. This usually involves a portion of your income—one-tenth or one-fifth, for example.

6. *The equal way.* Giving the same amount to the poor and God as we spend on ourselves.

7. *The heroic way.* Limiting our expenditures to just what we really need and giving away all the rest, no matter how much it might be.

Looking over the list, which category do you fall into?

Hit the Gas!

1. Which of the above are right ways of giving? Which are wrong ways? The best? The most glorious? Read Paul's prescription for giving in 1 Corinthians 16:1-2. Which methods of giving fall into his directive? _____

_____

_____

2. Which ways of giving do you think are possible? Is there any one in particular that appeals to you and might become a goal to shoot for? Which one? Why? _____

_____

_____

FRIDAY

You've Got to Be Kidding!

Another episode I want to tell you about happened in the year 1548 A.D. A young mother received an inheritance. Not a great sum, but it would have made her family very comfortable. Shortly thereafter a plague struck the city and many were without food and clothing. The woman wondered what she might do and decided, on the basis of the widow's story in Scripture, to use her inheritance to start a small bread, meat, and stocking ministry to the needy. She called it "The Widow's Purse." (Incidentally, I've noted some 16,024 individual works all over the world that were begun on the basis of the widow's story up until now.)

This woman was Martin Luther's wife. (Not that this should make any difference). She continued to influence others, including her husband, to help needy people—on the basis of the widow's gift in Scripture.

Michael, the stories go on and on. It's most gratifying to see what the Lord can do with only two lepta. This has been completely beyond normal record-keeping, but I'm glad we've kept up with it! (Note: In my next study I want to examine what God does with a whole *lifetime* of giving, good deeds, kind words, and prayers.)

The alarming thing I see in all this is what the widow hoped would happen with her lepta. As usual, I find that people—even the faithful—think in the sparest of terms. Her hope at the time was that her lepta might buy a brick for the Temple wall. Little did she know it would become a foundation sapphire in the New Jerusalem!

Pumpin' Premium

The "alarming thing" above is meant to be a warning. Do you ever find yourself dreaming small dreams, having little hopes, never really reaching for the stars? Why not start praying to reach the stars, to move the world, to have a tremendous impact on people for the kingdom of God?

It's wise to limit our prayers to what is real, of course. We shouldn't ask God to help us distribute tracts on the moon, or to make us rich so that we can give more. But what about. . .

- praying that God will enable you to give more, with the idea that you will eventually earn more so you can give more?

- praying that God will give you opportunities to reach more people for Christ, perhaps giving you the chance to give your testimony to hundreds or even thousands?

- praying that God will open a door that so far has been closed?

- praying that God will show you a special and new skill you can use for him?

Why not shoot for the stars and ask God to do more than we can ask or think about? In fact, that's how Paul put it in Ephesians 3:20: "Now to him who is able to do exceeding abundantly beyond all we can ask or think . . ."

During the early 1900s, a man in London named Emil Mettler often acted as a representative for Albert Schweitzer in the great doctor's writing and speaking ministries. He owned a restaurant in London and always gave a free meal to Christian workers when they stopped in. One time the secretary of the London Missionary Society had a fine meal in Mettler's restaurant and was standing at the cash register talking with Mettler, when he noticed a large nail lying among the bills. He asked what it was doing there, and Mettler said, "I keep this nail with my money to remind me of the price that Christ paid for my salvation and of what I owe him in return."

That's really the point of all giving, isn't it?

Hit the Gas!

1. Read Paul's eloquent words about Christ and what he longed to give him in return for his salvation in Philippians 3:1-14. What do you like about Paul's outlook? What can you apply to yourself? _____

_____

_____

2. What do you think would be the greatest motivation for you to give more than what you're giving now—especially if you realize it isn't in line with God's Word and will? Can you pray that God will give you that motivation? _____

_____

_____

WEEKEND

All That Money—Where Did It Go?

NOTE

Gabriel:

What were your findings on Zechariah?

Michael

MEMO

Michael:

Sorry to have failed to mention it. Zechariah, as you know, donated over a talent of silver, which is an awesome sum. (I didn't try to account for the exact figures, but let's just say it amounts to thousands of days wages). He wanted his gift used to purchase pillars in the main alcove of the Temple. This was precisely what he got. They purchased two pillars. And he had gold plates with his name on them affixed to the pillars. They stood for some forty years and were admired by many.

But as you know, a pillar doesn't do much to advance the kingdom of God, nor does it have any power to convert those who look upon it. (Zechariah didn't even affix a sign to the pillar to tell people about the gospel; however, his name was rather prominent.)

The Temple, as you know, was destroyed in 70 A.D. Really, only the Master knows exactly what happened to the pillars. (Records suggest that pieces of it went into a Roman roadbed and that the "gold plates" were discovered to be brass and were thrown out; Zechariah had been cheated by a Sadducee.)

As far as any rewards Zechariah would have received had he converted to the faith, there is no telling. I don't care to investigate possibilities.

Thanks for encouraging me to follow through on this.

Gabriel

Pumpin' Premium

Giving is a privilege for Christians, and should be entered into with joy. If you can't give with joy, perhaps you should pull back on your giving until you can; or perhaps you should give even more!

There is tremendous dignity made possible when we give till it hurts. Think of that poor widow. What if Jesus had said to her, "Ma'am, we know how needy you are. You don't have to give this money. It's all you have to live on. The Lord understands."

Why did Jesus so applaud her sacrifice, especially when it was so overshadowed by the rich people's giving? Why didn't he just let her heartfelt desire be enough?

A true story may help illustrate Christ's reason for accepting the gift. The pastor of a church in Virginia learned from a deacon that a certain very poor member of the church gave four dollars a month, a tithe of her total income. The deacons felt strongly that this poor woman needed the money far more than the church did and they suggested that the pastor tell her she was relieved of her responsibility to give in that ministry. They were confident the Lord would understand her poverty and inability to give.

The pastor went to the woman and told her graciously that she didn't have to continue giving as she had. As he spoke, tears slid down the lady's cheeks. She said, "I want to tell you that you are taking away the last thing that gives my life dignity and meaning."

There is great dignity in giving sacrificially, even if it's only a little. God doesn't spurn even the smallest gifts. If our hearts are right, nothing we bring to him will be turned away or used for foolishness!

Hit the Gas!

1. Once again read the story of the widow in Mark 12:41-44. What new thoughts do you have on the passage? How can you become a giver like that widow? _____

_____

_____

2. We've looked at a hard issue. What thoughts do you have now on the subject of giving? Has your attitude changed in any way? What goal might you set before God in the area of giving?

_____

_____

_____

Note:

1. These sums are difficult to determine in modern dollars. The best way of calculation, though, is to take the drachma (or denarius) as one day's ordinary wages for a laborer. Making that equal to $64 at $8/hour for a typical day's wages, that would make a lepton equal to 50 cents (1/128th part of a denarius).

Week Six

The Long Walk

MONDAY

Climbing the Cliff

The instructor demonstrated how to tie in the belaying rope by wrapping it around their waists and then knotting it at the center just below the navel. He said, "This rope is your lifeline. It protects you as you climb. If you slip or even fall, the person holding the line at the top will rope you in. You'll never fall more than a few feet. No professional rock climber would ever climb without being tied to a secure point, either by a person at the top holding the rope, or by pins secured in the rock with pitons, bolts, and carabiners. We're just doing a hundred-foot rock climb. Nothing here will be overwhelming, but it will be demanding."

Brad Longacre shifted his weight nervously as he looked up at the cliff towering over his little group. He'd never done a rock climb before, and the prospect induced in him a nearly paralyzing fear.

"Scared?" Jenny Howard, Brad's girlfriend, poked him in the ribs playfully.

"No."

"Yes you are."

"A little."

Jenny grinned. She had long, beautiful brown hair pulled back in a pony tail, and glorious blue eyes. It was through her that Brad's sister had gotten involved in the youth group at church. He'd finally come himself, on a dare. When he met Jenny, he began attending eagerly. And finally, within the last year, he'd become a full-fledged Christian, really trying to walk with Christ by getting involved in church, Bible study, youth group, and biblical living. It was hard, but he enjoyed it most of the time.

When Jim Lynch, the youth leader, took the group for a "survival camp" in the Adirondacks, though, it turned out to be more than a lark. It really *was* survival. The culmination was the rock climb. Brad didn't want to look like a wimp. But he could hear wild drumming in his chest, like thunder.

Jenny poked him again. "Why don't you go first? Show us your stuff."

"I've never done this before, Jen."

"Neither has anyone else."

It didn't matter. The instructor pointed to Brad anyway. "All right, Longacre, let's see you do it."

Brad sighed unhappily, but stepped forward to be tied in.

Pumpin' Premium

This week we'll focus on an important aspect of living a full life as a Christian: learning to walk with Jesus Christ. The image of "walking" occurs over and over again in the Bible.

"But I say, walk by the Spirit and you will not carry out the desire of the flesh" (Galatians 5:16).

"If we live by the Spirit, let us also walk by the Spirit" (Galatians 5:25).

"I, therefore, the prisoner of the Lord, entreat you to walk in a manner worthy of the calling with which you have been called" (Ephesians 4:1).

"Walk in love, just as Christ also loved you" (Ephesians 5:2).

"Be careful how you walk, not as unwise men, but as wise" (Ephesians 5:15).

Why did Paul use the image of walking as a picture of spiritual life? Consider several reasons:

1. Walking, like growing, moves you in a direction and gets you from point A to point B over a period of time.

2. Walking is natural—it's effortless for most of us.

3. Walking can be done with many other activities—talking, eating, playing.

4. Walking is a naturally inclusive activity: we can do it alone or with others and still engage in conversation.

God used the image of walking to help us picture our relationship with him as a journey, a movement from childhood to adulthood in terms of Christian growth. Most of all, Jesus walked *with* his disciples, teaching them as he walked from village to village, pointing out sights and using them as illustrations of what he wanted them to know and understand.

Think of your relationship with Jesus as a walk. What can you do on a walk that makes it a good way to relate to someone else?

Hit the Gas!

1. Read Galatians 5:16. What does this passage mean by "walking in the Spirit?" How does that relate to the cliff-climbing that is going on in the story? _____
_____
_____

2. How is your relationship with Christ like a walk? List several elements of Christian growth that are like walking. _____
_____
_____
_____

TUESDAY

On the Way Up

The climb didn't offer any easy spots, though there were plenty of places to get handholds and footholds. The belaying rope dangled slightly below him as he started the climb.

"Look and plan your way," the instructor said. "Keep looking up and ahead. There's no right path to take."

Brad stuck his hiking boot into the first toehold, reached up to a crevice, and pulled himself up.

"Go! Go! Go!" the group began to chant.

But the instructor yelled, "Quiet. He needs to think. Let him find his way. That's what the woods are all about: getting back to God's silence."

Right, Brad thought. *Just what I need*. A lengthy crevice lay just ahead. It was cut deeply along one horizontal layer about fourteen feet up. Brad couldn't see the man above, belayed in behind a big rock. "I hope he's staying alert," Brad murmured to himself.

The rope tightened slightly as Brad climbed. It gave him a feeling of confidence. His belay man was staying right in there with each step. He began climbing without thinking about the rope. He knew he wasn't to use it to help himself up over a projection or through a tough spot. But just the fact that it was there was a powerful assurance. He couldn't really hurt himself, he reasoned, even if he did slip—just as the instructor had said.

He was now ten feet up. A small chimney hung to his right, and to his left was an outcrop that he couldn't go over. He decided to try to work between the two.

"Be careful," he heard Jenny call up to him.

120

I am, I am, he said in his mind. *What do you think I'm doing?*

He scrabbled for leverage to pull himself up to a small ledge, then got a boot on it. Two more major rises and he would be over the top. He was already tired, though. Each lift and step took all his strength.

Pumpin' Premium

Here we are, talking about walking with Christ, relating to him on a kind of journeying basis, and yet I've used an illustration of kids making a rock climb as a metaphor for walking. How are they alike? How are they different?

Notice the belaying rope that is tied around the waist. That's protection for the climber so that if he falls, he won't fall to the ground below, but will be held up safely, free to restart his climb. What are some of the "securing lines" God has put into the Christian life to prevent us from falling and breaking our necks?

Consider this verse: "The steps of a man are established by the Lord, and He delights in his way. When he falls, he shall not be hurled headlong; because the LORD is the one who holds his hand" (Psalm 37:23-24).

Here is a picture of God holding our hand as we walk. It's the same principle as the belaying line on a rock climber. It's a form of security. God assures us that as we walk through this world, we can be sure we're not alone. He is there holding our hand. Or if that image makes you feel a bit too enclosed, think of the image of the shepherd and the sheep. He watches over us to ensure that no enemy attacks and hurts us. In the book of Job, Satan speaks of the "hedge" God had put around Job to protect him from assault. And in other passages, we read that God is like a rock, a shield, a fortress, an eagle, and a warrior.

All these images are designed to give us real security in life. Walking with Christ is meant to be a joyous adventure. But if we were constantly afraid of attack by Satan or others, that walk would generate little joy.

So God promises that he is with us and that he will never let go of our hand so that if we do fall, we won't be "hurled head-long."

Hit the Gas!

1. Read Psalm 37:24-25. What comfort does this passage give you? How does it make you feel about going into "enemy territory"—the real world where Christians are often rejected, mocked, or hated—to live out Christian principles? _____

_____

_____

2. What other passages in the Bible give us security? Why does God spend so much time in Scripture assuring us of the future and of his constant watchcare over us? _____

_____

_____

WEDNESDAY

Your Turn!

In another two minutes Brad was over it. Standing on the outcrop, he shielded his eyes from the sun. He had another thirty feet to go. But the instructor called up, "The rest is easy. Go to it!"

Brad soon ascended the final rise. He was greeted by the smiling face of one of the assistants. "Welcome," the man said. "You just made history."

"Yeah," Brad said. It was a good feeling. The instructor threw the rope back down to the group and called, "All clear. Number two ready to go."

Brad worked his way down the back side of the huge rock, which was steep, but not a climb requiring the assistance of another climber and a rope. He joined the rest of the group. One of his friends, Chuck Shirley, had begun to climb.

"How was it?" Jenny said.

"Exciting!"

"So you're gonna get into it—become the next free climber up the Matterhorn."

"No, I don't think so." Brad always enjoyed Jenny's subtle barbs. They both watched Chuck mount the outcrop and climb over the top. After a half-hour, two others had gone up, and two more climbs had been started at other points on the cliff.

"When're you going?" Brad asked Jenny, giving her a poke.

"Maybe next year," Jenny answered, not looking at him.

"Hey, no way. I did it. Let's get with the program."

Jenny turned to him. "I don't feel so good about this, Brad."

"Oh, try it. You can't get hurt."

"Yeah, that's what they all say."

Pumpin' Premium

Walking or climbing for Christ is something each of us has to do for ourselves. No one can do it for us. No, our walk with Jesus is ours alone. We do the walking *with* him, which means relating to him on a daily basis.

In the story you've been reading, Brad succeeded in climbing to the top of the rocks without mishap. It was a daring, low-risk free climb. But it stretched him. It caused him to do something he might have thought he couldn't do.

What are some of the risks involved in walking with Christ? Consider these:

- That he will require changes you might not want to make.
- That he will lead you into places where you might not normally wish to go.
- That he might bring others whom you don't like along on your walk with him.
- That you might have to face enemies of the faith, people who will make trouble for you as a Christian.

Before he was elected president of the United States, James Garfield was president of Hiram College. A man brought his son to Garfield, explaining that he wanted the boy to go to Hiram. The man asked that his son be allowed to take a shorter course of study so he could get out and work. "My son can never take all those studies," he explained. "He wants to get through more quickly. Can't you arrange for him to do that?"

"Oh, yes," Garfield answered. "He can take a short course; it all depends on what you want to make of him. When God wants to make an oak he takes a hundred years, but he only takes two months to make a squash."

Our walk with Christ is designed by God to make oaks, not squash, although I have to admit, fried with onions and peppers, squash isn't all that bad!

Hit the Gas!

1. Read the famous Psalm, chapter 23. What does this Psalm reveal about walking with Christ? Why do you think God pictures us as sheep and himself as a shepherd? _____

_____

_____

2. Why do you think walking with Christ can be so perilous at times? What is God's purpose in that, while protecting us, he sometimes lets us walk through "the valley of the shadow of death?" _____

_____

_____

125

THURSDAY

Tough Climb

Jenny started up at one of the easier climbs, on a pocked piece of rock-face that had plenty of handholds. She climbed with calm assurance. Brad liked watching her move. He thought she looked sexy, even though he hoped no one else noticed.

Jenny stopped at a small ledge to catch her breath. "This is really hard," she called down.

"Yeah, you have to be in good shape," the instructor said.

"She looks in pretty good shape to me," one of the boys commented.

"Yeah, I really like that rear-end action," another one said.

Brad grinned, and the girls just shook their heads.

Jenny set her foot in another notch and started up the rock-face again.

"Don't break a nail now," Brad called.

Jenny answered, "I've already broken three. I'm giving up on them." She was breathing hard.

The guy doing the belaying at the top was careful to keep the rope just tight enough to give her confidence, but loose enough to give her full freedom of movement as she climbed. Several times she looked down. Brad stared up at her and smiled. "You're doing all right."

"Yeah."

The most difficult part was just ahead—a wall about ten feet straight up. Brad watched as she planted a foot, got a handhold, then . . .

Pumpin' Premium

Using a belaying line while you climb has another effect besides providing security against a fall and physical harm. Properly used, the belay line is not kept tight but loose, just loose enough that the climber won't readily feel its presence. In effect, the climber mounts the rock without hindrance from the line. It's not "breathing down your neck" and reminding you it's there; it protects, but is not overbearing.

In the same way, Christ's presence as we walk with him is subtle. He doesn't hover over us trying to direct every little step and shuffle. He's not constantly pushing or pulling us to "get with the program." He gives us freedom to be ourselves.

The presence of the Spirit in our lives is meant to be a source of security—a ready voice to guide us through hard times. But he's also there as the person of Christ to be a friend.

A Jewish rabbi was asked by one of his students, "Why did God give the manna every day? Why didn't he give the people enough for a whole year so they wouldn't have to constantly go out and gather it?" The rabbi replied with a parable. "A certain king had a son to whom he gave a yearly allowance. Once a year the boy appeared in the throne room to get his due. But the king soon noticed that was the only day he ever saw his son. So he changed his policy. He switched from giving a huge lump sum on one day to giving him just the amount he needed for each day. Thus, the son visited his father every morning, and that gave each the time they needed to learn of one another and become true friends."

When using a belaying line, the climber is in constant touch with the man or woman above. As you walk with a companion, you relate moment by moment, friend to friend. God gave us the Spirit as an indwelling presence so we would feel his love moment by moment, continually. Yet at the same time, his presence is subtle, freeing; gently surrounding but not stifling; a caress, not a stranglehold.

Hit the Gas!

1. Read Romans 8:14-17. What does this passage teach about the Spirit's presence as we walk with Christ? _____

_____

_____

2. How does the Spirit make himself known to you? As you walk with Christ, how does that presence speak, move, act, guide, and teach? What is the most important aspect of God's presence in your life? _____

_____

_____

FRIDAY

Problems, Problems

The fall was sudden and harrowing. The belayer caught her within four feet and she swung out wildly from the cliff.

"Help!"

A second later, Jenny smacked against the wall of stone. The wind went right out of her. Everyone seemed to stop breathing.

"You okay?" the instructor called.

No answer.

Jenny hung at an odd angle, not moving. She was caught on a ledge, her leg under her.

"Jenny!" the instructor shouted. "Are you okay?"

Again no answer.

Immediately, the instructor called for another two lines.

"I'm going with you," Brad said.

"We'd better let experienced climbers handle this," the instructor replied.

"Please."

Giving him a hard look, the instructor said, "All right. Get tied in." He turned to one of the assistants. "Bill, you go up and belay Brad on the left. I'll take the right. I think she's just had a hard knock."

Brad's heart was pounding through his skull as he began climbing on the left side. He listened for any signs of Jenny coming out of it. But she hung there, limp. "Please, God, let her be all right," he prayed as he climbed.

Pumpin' Premium

Walking with Christ means a certain amount of adventure—perhaps even danger. You're going to have to face the reality of yourself and your sin in ways you never had to as an unbeliever. That's one kind of danger. Another kind is simply going into the "valley of the shadow of death," as Jenny did when she climbed the rock. Not that she necessarily was in much real danger. But there was always the chance of slipping, falling, hurting herself.

That's the third thing about climbing with a belaying line. Not only does it give you the security of knowing that you probably won't suffer serious harm, it also lets you be yourself, to go unhindered the way you want to go. If you study climbers, you'll see each has a "style," a way of scaling the mountain. One likes this route, another takes a different one. Each climber finds his own way to the top.

It's the same in your walk with Christ. Each of us has the freedom to develop his or her own style. For some, an organized quiet time where they can work right through the Bible is the best way. Others spend time with the Lord in the car on the way to work or school. Still others like to meditate on Scripture as they work on a project in art class or metal shop.

God doesn't want clones. He longs for each of us to develop and grow as individuals whom he can enjoy and delight in knowing as friends. If he'd wanted all of us to be exactly alike, he'd only have needed the original one. But God is a creator, the epitome of creativity. He's compelled to break the mold every time he fashions a new soul in the womb. Within certain limits, each of us has complete freedom to develop our walk with the Lord the way we want.

Yes, he wants us to know and live his Word. Yes, he wants us to pray. Yes, he's concerned that we be involved in ministry, serving, and church.

But at the same time, he lets us be individuals, allowing us to "strut our stuff." None of us needs to be a copy of anyone else.

What David says in Psalm 139:13-14 is appropriate here: "For Thou didst form my inward parts; Thou didst weave me in my mother's womb. I will give thanks to Thee, for I am fearfully and wonderfully made." God made you the only one of a kind. Your relationship and walk with him are the same.

Beware of getting locked into one pattern of relating to Jesus. As you grow in Christ, try new things, new ideas. Don't get stuck in a rut of overused processes. Learn to relate to him person-to-person.

That means no two moments have to be the same.

Hit the Gas!

1. Read Psalm 139:13-16. What does this passage reveal about our uniqueness and how being created in God's image involves individuality, personality, and a personalized walk for each of us? _____

_____

_____

2. What elements of your walk are unique? What you do and how you do things have your stamp on them. Name a few things that make you unique in this respect. _____

_____

_____

WEEKEND

Making It

When they reached her, the instructor propped Jenny up against the wall and held some smelling salts under her nose. She awoke with a start.

"Oh, my head!"

The instructor looked into her eyes. "You feel okay? No broken bones?"

Jenny took a quick inventory and said, "No, I don't think so."

"Then let's get you down. Just let him wind out the line and you'll go right down, no problem."

Jenny glanced at Brad. "No, I want to go on."

"You were knocked out, Jenny. You need to be on the ground," the instructor said.

"But if I'm okay, you'll let me try again?"

Brad said, "Jen, you don't have to do it."

"I know. I want to. It's a challenge."

The instructor said, "Let's get you down and make sure everything's okay."

Once on the ground, it was discovered that Jenny had a lump on the back of her head but was otherwise all right. After a half-hour rest while others tried the climb, she went again. This time Brad climbed next to her. "We can find footholds and handholds together."

Jenny laughed. "It'll be fun."

They climbed over the top together.

"See," Brad said, "this is more fun when you've got a babe next to you climbing the mountain."

"Yeah," Jenny said. "And I got to hang under your armpits several times."

Brad laughed. "Did they smell?"

"Was it Ice Blue Secret or Right Guard?"

Pumpin' Premium

There may be times in your spiritual growth and walk that you feel you've failed. There will undoubtedly be moments when you rebel, or sin, or even give up and leave the Christian life for a while.

Those reactions are all part of being human. God understands that we're prone to have problems and make mistakes. He doesn't condemn us when we blow it. Like Paul says in Romans 8:1-2, "There is therefore now no condemnation for those in Christ Jesus. For the law of the Spirit of life in Christ Jesus has set you free from the law of sin and of death." There is great freedom to fail in the kingdom of God. We need not condemn ourselves or let others condemn us. Try, try again is the name of the game in Christian living. If something doesn't work for you, leave it and try something else. As the saying goes, "Different strokes for different folks."

Do you feel as if someone is trying to lock you into a discipling or "growth" process that hems you in? Remember the lessons of the belay line. You should be able to:

1. *Feel secure as you grow,* just as the belaying line gives you security.

2. *Feel no hindrance in the methods that appeal to you,* just as the belay line should be loose enough to give you freedom to go in different directions as you desire.

3. *Feel completely yourself in the process.* The belay line is meant to be a help, not a hindrance. Your relationship with Christ should have your own stamp of individuality all over it. God isn't going

to put you into a box, just as he doesn't want you to put him in one.

Charles Kettering—a famed inventor of the early 20th century, founder of huge companies like Delco, and a partner in the founding of General Motors Corporation—said, "If you're doing something the same way you have been doing it for ten years, the chances are you are doing it wrong."

While there is much to be said for certain traditions—like Bible reading, prayer, sharing your faith, serving in church, and so on—there is also much to be said for finding fresh ways to carry out old practices. Jenny tried again and made her own way up the mountain. Similarly, every Christian should bring to his relationship with Jesus all of his own ideas for making it work. Step out on your own. Try something different. Get your fingerprints all over it. Let God show you a new way that might one day become one of the "old ways" for others!

Hit the Gas!

1. Read 2 Peter 3:18. What does this passage command us to do? What does it imply about growth in Christ? What do you think are the most important methods for growth? _____

_____

_____

2. Think of two new ways of doing the "old things" that longtime Christians speak about. Why not try one in your own walk today? _____

_____

_____

Week Seven

What to Do with Your Life Now

"HI, TOM! HEY, COULD YOU DO ME A LITTLE FAVOR AND ON OUR WAY
TO DINNER DROP OFF MY GRANDMOTHER AT K-MART, TAKE MY LITTLE
BROTHER AND HIS SICK TURTLE TO THE VET, RUN MY COUSIN STU TO
THE TRANSMISSION SHOP IN HURLEYSVILLE, TAKE MY...."

MONDAY

A Modest Complaint

I'm so sick of seeing the bad guys win. Yeah, I know how it happens in the movies. Steven Seagal or Jean-Claude Van Damme or Sylvester Stallone wipe everybody out against incredible odds. But it isn't that way in real life. Real life means even the good guys can turn out to be bad guys, the bad guys turn out to be *really* bad guys, and the really good guys ultimately give up or get whacked in the process.

I know I could spend most of my time being depressed about this, but what are you going to do? Depression is nowhere. Dropping out is *less* than nowhere. Hanging in there is all you can do. But sometimes it's like you're hanging by your thumbs, with six thousand feet of sheer cliff below you.

I see it every day. Like that kid down the street. What's his name—Jimmy? Just a kid in the neighborhood, and I live in a fairly decent one. But something was going on between a couple of gangs, I guess; there was gunfire, and Jimmy caught a slug in the chest. Dead on impact. Yeah, a great shot—to the wrong kid.

Man, I hate it. I really hate it. The principal at school tries to be tough. He has no idea what goes on in the bathrooms, locker rooms, outside in the parking lot. They try. I know they really try.

And then there's . . .

Oh, no, there's Mrs. Chambers' cat again. Up a tree. Such a stupid cat, and Mrs. Chambers out there trying to get him down. Ridiculous.

"Hey, Mrs. Chambers, need some help?"

"It's my little Jeremy again, Jeff. It's a good thing you're always around."

"Just after school, Mrs. Chambers."

"I know, I know. Can you climb up and get him? He's smart enough to get up there, but not smart enough to get down. Didn't pass his SATs."

I had to laugh. Getting the cat is so simple. I wish everything was this easy. Well, guess I gotta climb a tree. See you in about ten minutes.

Pumpin' Premium

Hollywood aside, it's a rough world. Getting a job, getting through school, being nice to rude, outrageous-behaving people—it's tough. I know how Jeff feels. I've been there. How about you?

Look around. Read the paper. What do you see? Killing. Tax hikes. The government doing little in your neighborhood. Potholes everywhere. Classes that don't have the right equipment—or any equipment. Teachers who can't, or just don't, teach.

I sympathize. I've sat through more than a few boring classes. I've gotten bad grades from a teacher who knew less than I did. I've seen kids get into fights and get mauled.

What do you do?

Here's a word from Paul: "For we are his workmanship, created in Christ Jesus for good works, which God prepared beforehand, that we should walk in them" (Ephesians 2:10). What is this verse telling us? We are God's *workmanship*. Each of us is custommade. God's "man for the planet." God's "woman for our time."

And what were we created for? Good works.

I can hear it now. "Look, Buster, I'm no goody-goody."

We're not talking about being "goody-goody." Just doing *good works*.

Like what?

Start with Mrs. Chambers' cat—the classic way to do a good work, next to being a Boy Scout and helping a little old lady across the street. It's simply a matter of doing good whenever and wherever you can.

Not too tough, right? It's only a matter of the will, right?

Correct. That's all it is. Just choosing to do good when the opportunity arises.

And what else does Ephesians 2:10 say? "Good works, which God prepared beforehand, that we should walk in them."

In other words, not only did God create us for good works, but he actually arranged that we would have plenty of opportunities come our way in the normal run of the day.

We tend to think that "good works" are the stupendous things—the man who talks a guy down from the fourteenth-floor ledge, or plucks a baby from the street moments before a dump truck flashes by.

No, good works are the little things of life. Helping Mom with the dishes. Letting your sister watch what she wants to watch on TV. Stuff like that. Samuel Johnson once said, "He who waits to do a great deal of good at once, will never do a thing."

Amen. It's doing what's there now that counts in the eyes of God. Like a cat up a tree in Mrs. Chambers' yard.

Hit the Gas!

1. Read and think about Ephesians 2:10. Can you think of several opportunities to do good works that God gave you today? What were they? What did you do? _____

_____

_____

2. Can you think of an opportunity you might have missed today? How might you be on the lookout for them tomorrow?

_____

_____

_____

TUESDAY

Doing What Comes Along

So you see, the way I figure, it's that everybody's out for himself. Oh, I guess there are a few people here and there who aren't just after money or sex or drugs or whatever. But I haven't seen many of them. Even the people at church. Yeah, a lot of them are sincere and decent folks, and many of them would probably give you the shirt off their back. But in most cases it's not my style of shirt, know what I mean?

Now don't get me wrong. I'm not down on the church, or God, or Jesus. I believe in Jesus and I've been a Christian for a few years now, so I've been around a little. But people at church—most of them come in from out in the suburbs—all they want is to stay in their homes and have peace and no major disturbances; just be quiet and nice and everything'll be okay.

To some degree they're right, too. God doesn't want us mixing in trouble for the sake of the trouble. But we were called to be *witnesses*. To do something in the world. If all God wanted was for us to be saved, then why doesn't he just whisk us outta here the moment we make the decision? Because I figure he wants us to do something *besides* get saved—or even witness, or read the Bible, or pray, which is stuff we're all supposed to do anyway. So I feel like there has to be a lot more to it.

Uh, oh, here's Mom. Gonna be another list, I bet.

"Jeffrey, are you writing on that computer of yours again?"

"Yes, Mom."

"Did you do the things I asked you?"

"What were they?"

"Clean up your room. Organize the videos in alphabetical order. And vacuum the living room."

"Done, Mom."

"Do I need to inspect?"

"Be my guest."

"If I find anything still undone, you're in trouble, mister."

"Sure, Mom."

It makes me laugh. Mom tries to be tough, but she's a cream puff. Anyway, let me finish my lunch here—put the plate and glass in the washer; put the bologna away; stash the Coca-Cola. Presto! I'm done.

"Jeff, can you help me with this problem?"

My little brother. Well, be talking to you later.

Pumpin' Premium

A minister was walking down the street in a district with huge Victorian homes. It was bitterly cold, and a foot of snow lay on the neatly dressed-out lawns. Looking around, he saw a little boy trying to reach the doorbell on the porch of one of the houses. It was one of those old-time type doorbells, high on the door, and the boy was very short. He obviously couldn't reach it. After jumping a few times, he would stop and blow on his hands. It was freezing cold.

Poor kid, thought the minister, *I should help him.* He went up onto the porch, patted the boy on the head, and said, "Need some help?"

"Sure," the boy said.

The minister rang the bell vigorously. "Well . . . now what, my little friend?"

The kid looked up at him with a sly smile. "Now, run like the devil!" With that he wheeled and took off down the street. At the same time, the door opened and an elderly woman in spectacles said, "Can I help you?"

Trying to do good doesn't guarantee success. Our friend Jeff in the story above isn't getting scammed like the minister is. And to be honest, Jeff is a pretty good kid. He helps. He doesn't complain that much. And he's usually willing to do what comes along.

But what about another issue? What about making opportunities? Sure, Jeff has a lot of stuff coming at him. He's got plenty of problems to fix. But what about him going out there and making things happen?

Doing good isn't just helping out when the opportunity arises. It's getting out there and doing all you can to make things happen. How? Look for needs out there that you might not normally notice.

Some time ago there was a "Local Heroes" column in our daily newspaper. It featured local kids and adults who went out of their way to help needy people. Several guys in high school began mowing lawns—no charge—for several elderly women who didn't have the money to pay. In the winter, they also shoveled snow for the ladies—again, for free.

Other groups went and gathered free food for the poor— food of a kind most people didn't want. So they worked out a deal to sell it to another group. With the money, they bought the kind of food some of the local poor families really wanted—and needed.

It's not difficult. Keep your eyes open. Do what you can where you can. And start thinking in terms of making things happen. So what can you do today that might open a door of opportunity?

Hit the Gas!

1. Read Galatians 6:9-10. Why do you think Paul had to remind the Galatians about this? Is it something we all need to be reminded of? Why? _____

_____

2. Do we have to wait for opportunity to happen, or can we make it happen? How? What are some opportunities you might make happen today? _____

_____

WEDNESDAY

Sharing What Really Counts

So, where were we?

I don't want to come off as a complainer, okay? I mean, I'm not really down on people in general. So please don't pin that one on me. It's just that I'm tired of, well . . . of nothing big happening, I guess. I mean, I always thought that when I joined up with God, some heavy stuff was going to start raining down.

Like what?

Well, first of all, I thought I'd be leading a lot of people to Christ. All over the place. Wherever I went. I'd just give kids at school or on the street the gospel and suddenly they'd just turn to him, right then and there.

You know what happened? Most of my friends stopped being my friends. Why? Because I wouldn't gamble with them, do drugs, or use girls. Not that I was really into those things before. In fact, when I became a Christian I was kind of young, so I never was into those things at all.

But here's the problem: As my friends grew older, they *did* start to do those things. And when I refused, well, that was the end of the friendship.

I do hang out with some of the Christian dudes around. Life is better in a lot of ways because of that. But somehow it's not the same. The kids I grew up with, the ones I loved and cared about—I'd really like to see *them* come to Christ, too.

Right now, I'm sitting here in this doctor's office, waiting to see the doc. Problem with—well, I'm not going into that. You'd think I was being gross. Anyway. . .

"Sonny, do you have the time?"

"Yes, ma'am. It's 4:15."

"Thank you. Seems all I do is wait in doctors' offices these days."

"I know the feeling."

"No, you don't. You're young, sonny. But I'm old. I don't have much time left."

I looked into her eyes a moment. It was just her and me. So I decided to go for it.

"I found a way to live forever, ma'am. You wanna hear about it?"

"You're not one of those religious fanatics, are you?"

"No, just the mild brand."

"Well, I'm not sure about this. But I am getting old. . ."

"This would be a great time to hear about it."

Pumpin' Premium

Mark Twain, the author and humorist of the late nineteenth century, liked to play practical jokes. One time he went to the races and met a friend there who had lost everything on the betting. Twain himself had not done well. The friend commented, "I'm broke. If someone would buy me a ticket, I could go home on the train."

Twain said, "Well, I'm nearly broke myself. But I'll tell you what to do. You can hide under my seat and I'll hide you with my legs."

The friend thought it might work. Meanwhile, Twain went to the ticket office and bought *two* tickets, one for himself and one for his friend. When the train pulled out of the station and the conductor came by to see the tickets, Twain handed them both to him. "Where's the other one?" the conductor asked.

Tapping his head to indicate someone had "mental problems," Twain said in a loud voice, "That is my friend's ticket. He's a little eccentric and likes to ride under the seat."

Even when you're doing good, you can keep a sense of humor about it. In fact, someone's humor can ease the tension of being on the receiving end of a good deed—a "person in need." People don't always like to be helped because they're suspicious of strangers who are willing to lend a hand. That is especially true of sharing the gospel.

But sharing the faith is the ultimate good to offer to a needy world. It just needs to be tempered with other forms of goodness, friendship, and decency. Missionaries learned long ago that if the natives are hungry, they will not listen to the gospel until they're fed. Mission organizations discovered that by bringing in food, medical supplies, farming equipment and tools, people were much more willing to listen to their message.

How do you think Jeff is doing? There isn't a whole lot he can do to help this person, but he does "make an opportunity" by reaching out. What ways might he continue to befriend this person and possibly make a friend for Christ?

Hit the Gas!

1. Read in Romans 1:11-15 about Paul's attitude toward sharing the gospel. Why did Paul so want to share the gospel with the Romans? What burned in him and why? What were his thoughts about that sharing? Did he see himself as the "great teacher" coming to help the lost pagans? How did he view his role? _____

_____

_____

2. Why is sharing the gospel a form of doing good? What good do you do when you help others in this way? Read James 5:19-20. _____

_____

_____

THURSDAY

More Problems Popping Up

She didn't accept the Lord, but she listened. That's more than a lot of people will do.

Anyway, I'm on the way home from the doctor's office, and...

Would you look at that. A Christmas tree lying in the middle of the street. People are weaving around it. I don't know why these things happen to me. Guess I'll just stop and pull it over to the side of the road.

Well, that felt good. My good deed for the day.

Anyway, like I was telling you, I'm not really fed up. Or even disillusioned. Just kind of tired of seeing evil win all the time. I wish God would get in there and break some thug's arms, know what I mean? I mean really bash up Satan and his groupies. But I guess that's reserved for the end times—when God *really* wallops some of the bad dudes around.

But I just wish he'd do something now.

Hey, look at that kid! Biking right across the street without looking either way. What an...

"Hey, you. Idiot-kid."

"What you want, man?"

"You want to get killed or something?"

"Not really."

"Then be careful. Look before you cross."

"Who are you, God or somethin'?"

"No, but I'm a friend of his."

"Yeah, right."

Kids. I mean, I'm only a few years older'n him, but even *I* had more sense than kids these days. They think they own the universe. Like nothing can happen to them; they're invincible. Like they believe the stuff they see on Saturday morning cartoons.

Oh well. Who am I? Am I going to change the world? Like I'm somebody, know what I mean? Even the president of the country can't do much these days.

Anyway, got to stop here and get some Fruity Pebbles for my brother and sister. Mom asked me to pick some up on the way home. Fruity Pebbles—the greatest cereal. Ever try it?

I hate standing in lines, but at least I can try to memorize a Scripture while I'm here. . . Finally, the lady's gonna take my money!

"Will this be all?"

"Yes. Just the Fruity Pebbles."

"Do you have a coupon?"

"No. Just cash."

"Here's your change."

I look at it. "Hey, I gave you a ten, not a twenty."

"Oh, boy, am I in a daze. Thanks."

Man, and to think I coulda made an easy ten bucks. That's five video rentals . . . Oh well, what's right is right.

Pumpin' Premium

Another way to do good is simply to be honest. Someone gives you the wrong change—in your favor—and you choose to do right. You give back the extra money.

Or, when you could tell a lie and get out of a sticky spot, you tell the truth instead. Maybe you get nailed with a ticket or some other penalty, but you were honest. God honors that.

It can be tiresome. You get sick of always being the honest one when you see so many others do wrong and get away with it. Or so it seems. Keeping to the speed limit can invite criticism, even scorn, from friends. But obeying the traffic laws is a form of doing good that many of us overlook.

The author of Hebrews said, "Obey your leaders, and submit to them . . . as those who will give an account" (Hebrews 13:17). Paul said, "Let every person be in subjection to the governing authorities" (Romans 13:1). And, "Owe nothing to anyone except to love one another; for he who loves his neighbor has fulfilled the law" (Romans 13:8).

A way to show love, and to obey your leaders and the law, is to do good everywhere you go. You pick up a piece of trash in your path and dump it into a bin. You give a smile to a harried school worker or janitor, offering a kind word when you could just pass on by. You jump in to help when you'd rather just keep on going. All these are ways to do good and help others that cost little but a choice.

Sidney Poitier, famous star of such films as *In the Heat of the Night, They Call Me Mister Tibbs,* and *To Sir with Love,* was not always the eloquent, masterful speaker he became. When he first came to the U.S. from the Bahamas, he worked in an Astoria, New York restaurant as a dishwasher. Each night as the waiters had their 11 P.M. dinner, after the restaurant closed, Poitier would have to wait around so he could wash their dishes. He often read from a newspaper, trying to improve his very elementary reading skills. One night he asked one of the Jewish waiters what a certain word meant. After telling him the meaning, the waiter asked, "Do you run across many words you don't understand?" Poitier answered, "A lot. I'm just beginning to learn to read well." As a result, the waiter began coaching him every night.

In his memoir, *This Life* (Knopf), Poitier wrote, "This soft-spoken, natural teacher, with thick bifocals, bushy eyebrows, and silver-white hair, sat with me night after night and gave me a little piece of himself. I don't know if he's alive or dead now—but a bit of him is in everything I do."

It was a small way to help an uncertain man on his way up the rungs of life. But every little bit counts. The people we help

today may not end up in the news or write a biography that pub-
licly thanks us, but God himself will reward us in heaven. He
says, "Whatever you do, do your work heartily, as for the Lord. . .
knowing that from the Lord you will receive the reward of the
inheritance" (Colossians 3:23-24).

Hit the Gas!

1. Read Colossians 3:22-25. What does this passage offer by
way of counsel about doing good in your work and all else you
do? _____

_____

_____

2. Do we get any immediate reward for doing good in daily
life? What? How? Can you give an example from your own life?

_____

_____

_____

FRIDAY

Doing Something Stupendous

It's just that I want to see God work; *you* know. I mean, really blow this world to pieces. Not literally, but make some people—everybody—stand up and take notice. Why doesn't he do something so stupendous the world just goes wild?

It's kind of like I want Jesus to come back.

Hey, that's funny, because he *is* going to come back. And when he comes he'll blow the world's mind, to use an old expression. So to some degree, God has already told me he's gonna do the very thing I'm asking for. It's just that I wish he'd hurry up and do it! Really sack these bad guys. Knock them flat!

I'd like to be part of it, too. You know, be there when it happens. I'd like to see people like Castro, and those Nazi skinheads in Germany, and Saddam Hussein really get theirs! That is, unless they repent.

All right, now I'm getting personal. But I guess it comes down to. . .

Uh oh, some old guy just spilled his groceries in the street. And look at that—somebody drove over his grapefruit. Why do I have to have a conscience?

"Say, mister, you need a hand?"

"I'm hurtin', son. That was my last ten dollars."

"Here, let me help you pick the stuff up. There, everything's back in the bag. Where you goin' with these?"

"Just down the street—two blocks. There. There's my house."

"You need a ride?"

"I could use one."

Two minutes later we were there.

"Here, I'll help you in . . . . Pretty run-down in here."

"Don't have any money. Social Security barely pays the bills."

"Well, say, my church has a special fund for people who could use a little help. Would you like me to have you put on the list?"

"They're not one of those places that comes and visits you all the time, are they, and wants you to join?"

"Well, they'll visit you if you want. But no, it's just a special fund to help people without much money."

"Sure, okay."

Pumpin' Premium

A kindly old man helped a boy push an overloaded cart up a steep hill. As they both stood at the top, breathing heavily, the old man said angrily, "Only a scoundrel would expect a youngster like you to do a job like that! Your employer should have known it was too heavy for you."

"He did," answered the boy, "but he said, 'Go on, you're sure to find some old fool who'll help you up the hill.' "

Well, what do you do with that? Are we all "old fools" when we offer a hand? Are we goody-goodys, people with Superman complexes?

Yes, the world will laugh at us at times. Our friends will think we're weird. They'll get exasperated if our doing good gets in their way or messes up their schedule. But what's life for if you can't go out and do something decent for people as often as you can? So what if they call you "Boy Scout." So what if they laugh at you behind your back. You know who you serve. Don't you?

Remember Paul's words in Galatians 6:9: "Let us not lose heart in doing good, for in due time we shall reap." One day we'll reap a rich harvest for our labors.

But we have to keep our eyes on the truth, the Word of God, not on what the world says. The world honors and talks up those who are tough—"lean and mean" and all that. The guy who "is nobody's patsy" often ends up a hard-hearted, miserable old buzzard whom no one wants to be around.

When I served as a pastor, I repeatedly had people come to my church with long, sad tales of misery and difficulty. We sometimes gave those people hundreds of dollars to help them get back on their feet. Afterward, though, I occasionally found out that someone I helped was a con artist who literally made a living by ripping off churches like mine. You might think those experiences would have embittered me against all people who came around looking for financial help. But I honestly wasn't daunted.

I knew a certain percentage of people would take advantage of our love and our willingness to help. That kind of thing shouldn't stop us from trying to help others. God knows our heart. I'm certain that if we do someone a good turn in good faith, even if that person turns out to be a con man or bad guy, he'll still reward what was in our heart.

Hit the Gas!

1. Read Jesus' words in Matthew 10:16. How does this truth relate to helping others? _____
_____
_____

2. Have you ever been conned? How did it make you feel? What do you think is a biblical reaction to such acts of sin? _____
_____
_____

WEEKEND

Coming Full Circle

I like helping people. Sure. It's fun. It makes me feel good. But I still wish God would do something truly razzle-dazzle, know what I mean?

No, I guess you don't.

Oh boy, there's Mrs. Chambers with her cat again.

"Just let me get the groceries in the house, Mrs. Chambers. I'll get the kitty down."

"Thanks, Jeffie."

It seems like I've got a never-ending list of things to do, places to go, and people to help. *Does* it ever end?

"Mrs. Chambers, just stand there now and I'll go up the tree, okay?"

"Be careful, Jeff."

"Here, kitty, kitty. Now don't go out on the branch too far. . . Hey, I'm trying to help you, fella. . . Mrs. Chambers, tell him not to go out there."

"Jeremy. Jeremy, honey. Go to Jeffrey. Go into his arms."

"Sure hope this branch doesn't break. Come here, Jeremy. Just come right here. Hey, did you hear that?"

"Get back! Get back, it's going to . . ."

"Ahhhhhhhhhhh!"

"Jeff! *Jeff!* Wake up! Are you all right?"

Man, what a headache. Was I asleep or something? Was I dreaming?

"Jeff, wake up! You hit your head on the sidewalk. Are you all right?"

"Not with you shaking me like that, Mom. Hi, Mrs. Chambers. Oh, I see Jeremy's okay."

"Now don't move, honey. You may have broken something!"

"I'm all right, Mom. Just let me stand up."

So that's it. My day. A beaut, wasn't it?

Pumpin' Premium

A church newsletter recorded this saying: "There is a vast difference between putting your nose in other people's business and putting your heart in other people's problems."

When you do good, you may end up getting hurt. There are risks associated with helping others. Policemen know that one of the most dangerous situations to step into is a family argument. Officers are advised to be very careful in such situations. When an officer goes in to help a woman or man in conflict with a relative, sometimes the policeman, coming as a peacemaker, ends up being shot.

In fact, Solomon said in one of his proverbs, "Like one who takes a dog by the ears is he who passes by and meddles with strife not belonging to him" (Proverbs 26:17).

Jeff's situation doesn't exactly qualify as meddling in strife that is not his own. He's just helping get a cat out of a tree. But this story does illustrate the fact that there are risks in doing good. In rescue attempts and other dangerous situations, people who try to help others in distress are hurt and even killed. It's all a matter of using your head, thinking clearly, and being cautious any time you try to help others. In a truly dangerous situation, it's often wise to let professionals get involved instead of risking your life.

Most of the time, though, we're not facing situations in life that threaten us with serious harm. For most of us, it's just giving others our best as often as we can.

People will use us, con us, mistreat us as Christians and even scorn us for our doing good. But as Paul said, "Do not grow weary in well-doing" (2 Thessalonians 3:13). No matter how hard it is, no matter who uses you, love, give, serve, share, help . . . as much as you can. One day God will reward you.

Hit the Gas!

1. Why do we "grow weary in well-doing" as Paul says in 2 Thessalonians 3:13? What motivates you not to grow weary? What words of the Bible encourage you? _____

_____

_____

2. Think through today. What good were you able to do? What reward did you get for that good? How do you feel about it now? Was it worth it? Why, or why not? _____

_____

_____

Week Eight

To Glorify God and Enjoy Him Forever

MONDAY

Grandfather and I

I watched Grandfather walk wearily up the street toward
me as I sat on the stoop of his small stone house. I couldn't help
but think of how he had spoken that morning in worship.
Friends. He had called us "friends of Jesus." It was a new expression. I'd never heard him use it before. But so many new things
were a part of his teaching these days.

I wanted to ask him about it. After all, I was thirteen now—a
man.

Well, maybe not *quite* a man. Not like Grandfather.

Grandfather always listened to my questions and answered
well. I remember years back, when I was five or six, sitting on
Grandfather's lap as he taught the church at Ephesus. Grandfather had been one of them, one of the first—a disciple of Jesus.
That always made me feel a little proud. I know we Christians
aren't supposed to say such things. But I *am* proud of it. I don't
know why he always claims that being one of the original disciples provides no special advantage. He says we *all* have the Spirit.
And the ones who are truly blessed are those who didn't see
Christ and yet believed. Grandfather says Jesus said that himself.

But Grandfather knew Jesus as few others ever knew him.
As a man. As a leader. As a carpenter. They were cousins, and
probably played together when they were young.

To me, it seems like something that happened centuries
ago—but it was Grandfather's boyhood. I wish I had been there
too. Friends. That was it. They'd been *friends*.

Pumpin' Premium

In the *Westminster Shorter Catechism*, a teaching device used since the 1600s to help Christians understand the basics of our faith, the question is asked, "What is the chief end of man?" In other words, what is mankind's whole purpose in life? The short answer: "That we may glorify God and enjoy him forever."

Pretty simple. Glorifying God is simply recognizing God's true worth and greatness in every aspect of life. Enjoying him is—well, *enjoying* him.

Sometimes that seems hard to do. How do you consciously choose to enjoy God? I mean, either you do or you don't, right? It's not something you can make happen. It's something that happens to you. In the midst of a situation—a party, gathering, personal moment, whatever—we suddenly realize, "Hey, I'm enjoying this." Isn't it kind of the same thing with God? It either happens or it doesn't. But we don't think of it as something that we're supposed to *make* happen.

Well, put it in another context. Suppose you were asked, "What is the chief end of watching an Indiana Jones movie?" Answer: "That you might have fun and enjoy the picture for its duration."

That's simple enough. What about, "What is the purpose of school?" Answer: "That you might learn the basic truths and facts of living and apply them accordingly."

Take it to another level: "What is the purpose of marriage?" Answer: "That you might love and enjoy and get pleasure and fulfillment from one another till death do you part."

In the same way, God wants us to enjoy our relationship with him. How does that happen? In the context of relating. As we get to know him, learn of him, sit at his feet and grow, as we praise him and love him, we find that we actually *enjoy* him. Just like we enjoy having a favorite uncle come to visit. Or a date with a girlfriend or boyfriend. The enjoyment occurs in the process of relating.

There is a story of a Roman emperor who paraded through the streets of Rome as he returned from an incredible military victory in the north. Legionnaires lined the lanes as the chariots passed. At one end of the street was a majestic platform on which sat the royal family. As the emperor drew near, his youngest son spotted him and jumped off the platform, wormed through the throng, and attempted to run out to the lead chariot. A guard caught him, though, saying, "You can't do that. Don't you know who's in that chariot? That's the emperor."

The boy shouted, "He may be your emperor, but he's *my* father."

Like that son and father, God is personal to all of us. You can run to him and know he will give you all of his divine attention, as if you were the only person on Earth.

Hit the Gas!

1. One of the best pictures of how personal God can be is drawn in Psalm 23. Read it again and comment on the parts of it that reveal the ways in which we enjoy God and God enjoys us.

_____

_____

_____

2. Name one element of God's person that you most enjoy. Why did you pick this one? Can you show how that truth has touched your life, how God himself has touched you? _____

_____

_____

TUESDAY

The Friend

Grandfather smiled as he walked up to the boy. *Grandfather is always so full of joy,* thought Israel. *Sometimes I wish I could be like that. But his face is creased now; wrinkles line the corners of his eyes and mouth. He's been in many battles during his long life. He is one of the few who are left. How he grieved, Mother said, when James was behead-ed. Later, Peter, Thomas, Philip—all are gone now. Even Paul, who hadn't been among the original twelve, but who had done much in Ephesus long ago, before I was born.*

"And how is my fine grandson this afternoon?" Grandfather asked, shading his eyes from the sun.

Israel rubbed his toe in the dirt of the street. "I have a question. About something you said this morning."

Grandfather's eyes lit up. "Just a quick drink of water and then we'll talk. Did you fill the jug?"

"It's in on the table."

"Give me a moment."

Grandfather disappeared through the doorway.

Israel thought about how he would phrase his question. His grandfather was always so particular about the way things were phrased, he knew. He tried to be so exact. *Sometimes you'd think it was him instead of Matthew or Paul who wrote all those letters,* the boy thought.

Israel heard his grandfather's heavy leather sandals on the tile floor. A moment later he groaned as he sat down next to him.

"You're tired?" asked Israel, though he already knew the answer.

"Just old bones," said Grandfather. "Now, what was your question?" He cupped a small clay drinking vessel in his hand.

"This morning you spoke of our being friends of Jesus. It made me think of something."

"Yes?"

"Well, in a special way, I guess, more than any of us, Jesus was your friend."

Grandfather laughed. "Israel, he is a friend for all of us. Also Lord, Master, King, and Savior to all—not just me."

"I know, I know. But you walked with him. You heard his voice. You spent nights and days with him in the hills. There must have been something special about it."

"Well, his voice was no different. . . "

"No, I don't mean that, Grandfather. It's not what His voice was like—though that would be interesting to know—but what *he* was like. As a person. As a. . ."

"Friend?"

"Yes."

The old man leaned back and looked up at the blue sky over Ephesus. *Being so near the sea is such an advantage,* he thought. *Cool breezes. And blue, blue skies.*

Pumpin' Premium

A little boy from the Midwest moved from Iowa to Nebraska. He ran into the house one day and asked, "How long is God, Mom?"

Somewhat confused by the question, the boy's mother said, "What do you mean?"

The boy answered, "When we lived in Iowa, you told me God was there with us. And now at school they say God is here in Nebraska, too. I know God can't be *that* long."

A chuckle aside, the story reveals a common truth. We get our ideas about God from many sources, and if we get the wrong information it can really destroy our image of the Creator. Some people picture God as a policeman, always laying down laws and then catching the sinners and punishing them. But Scripture clearly says we live, not by law, but by grace. If anything, God is the opposite of a hard-nosed, letter-of-the-law policeman type, being gracious, forgiving, loving, and understanding.

Some think of God as a fireman—the kind of person who only shows up when there are terrific problems, and then he might not get there until too late. But God says in Isaiah, "I will be with you in the fire" (Isaiah 43:2). And you may remember Shadrach, Meshach and Abednego in Nebuchadnezzar's furnace in the book of Daniel. God didn't put out the fire—as a fireman would do. No, he was *with* them in the fire.

Others picture God as a hanging judge—the kind of person who can't wait to get us into court and sentence us to death. But Jesus says he came "to seek and to save that which was lost" (Luke 19:10).

I've heard of people who think of God as a spy—always watching us and writing down all our sins and errors; or as a Santa Claus—an old, bearded gentleman who wants nothing more than to give us everything; or as a "killjoy"—the type of person who ruins a party every time.

But none of these are true pictures of God, even though people will sometimes find solitary Scriptures they can use out of context to "prove" their narrow view of God is correct.

The *whole* Bible is God's means of showing us what he is like. In it you see him as guide and leader (with Abraham), lawgiver (with Moses), judge (Samson), healer, miracle worker, and word-spinner (in the person of Jesus); instructor (through the letters of Paul), comforter and encourager (in the person of the Holy Spirit), and a hundred others. All of them are meant to give us a wide-lens view of our Lord and Master. Which ones most appeal to you?

Hit the Gas!

1. Look at the description of God in Psalm 145:1-5. Which aspects does the Psalmist zero in on as the crowning glories of God's nature? Which ones draw you? Why? _____

_____

_____

2. We've been looking at God as a friend. What do you think are components of God's person in Jesus that best illustrate how he was a friend to the disciples and is now a friend to us? _____

_____

_____

_____

WEDNESDAY

Water Into Wine

"There were so *many* things," Grandfather said. He laughed. "You know, sometimes it's very funny, the way things happened. Jesus never put himself before others. Of course, there was the Kingdom and his life's mission. I don't mean that. But sometimes he did things which at the time I so disagreed with. . ."

"Like what?"

"Oh, for instance, the time He changed water into wine at Cana. That was his first miracle. The *very* first."

"I've never heard of it."

"Not Matthew, Mark, nor Luke so much as mentioned it. I don't know why. But I remember it vividly. We went to the wedding of our mutual cousin in Cana. He was not well-to-do. But many people came. And stayed. It all went on and on. People were having such a fine time."

"Like at Uncle Josiah's wedding a year ago?"

"Yes. When you live under the kinds of pressure and conditions we did in Galilee in those days, a wedding was a first-rate chance to have some fun. And that's exactly what we did."

"I hope they weren't drunk."

"No, not drunk. But there was wine. Good wine. Levi bought the best, even though he couldn't afford it. And then they ran out."

"Oooh! That would be embarrassing. Even *I* know that." Israel felt a twinge of pride.

Grandfather nodded. "Yes, it was. And then Jesus' mother—she was Levi's aunt—went to Jesus. She always understood things before the rest of us did. She asked Jesus to help."

"What did Jesus do?"

"He didn't tell any of us. He simply gave some orders, and the next thing we knew, we had several baths of wine. Good wine. Light. Ruby-colored. The *best*."

"Even better than what they'd been drinking?"

"Yes."

"But why did he do that first? It seems to me he would have healed someone or done one of the greater miracles."

"That's just what I thought," Grandfather said with a smile. "But that was Jesus. He was a friend first—someone who thought of you and your needs. Like the way he always explained things to us, especially to me, James, and Simon. We could ask any question we wanted. Not like with the rabbis and scribes. If you would ask *them* something, they always scowled first, then would tell you that if you read the Scriptures, you wouldn't ask such silly things. Jesus wasn't that way."

Pumpin' Premium

Part of the way God expresses his friendship with us is by helping us in times of need, even situations like the above where Jesus turned water into wine at Cana. Have you felt God's help at times in your life? Have you sensed that he was present and close and working in a situation to protect or guide you?

A disciple named Felix of Nola was pursued by enemies because of his preaching of faith in Christ. Tired and fearful, he reached a cave and went inside, hoping his pursuers would miss him. As he lay inside, though, he noticed a spider as it began to weave a web across the mouth of the cave. He was stunned at the beauty and wonder of the spider's work, and had little thought of how God might be using it. However, when the people chasing him reached the cave, they saw the spider's web over the opening and decided to move on. If Felix were inside, he would have broken through the web, they reasoned. Felix was saved, and he later wrote, "Where God is, a spider's web is a wall; where he is not, a wall is but a spider's web."

Certainly there are times when all of us have experienced God's love and friendship through protection, a strange visitation of help, money, or food when we were in need, or just a sense of comfort when we were hurting. The God of the Bible is an intensely personal God, one who gets down in the dirt with us in the person of Jesus and shows us he is one of us.

Why does God so emphasize the personal aspects of his nature? Because he made us personal beings who never rest till we find our peace in him. Like St. Augustine, a writer of the fourth century, pictured it, there is a "God-shaped vacuum" in the heart of each person, a whole that God alone can fill.

One of the best pictures of his personal way of relating to us is found in Romans 8:16: "The Spirit Himself bears witness with our spirit that we are children of God." Through the Spirit, God makes himself real and personal to each of us. He becomes an indwelling presence, a friend who is literally inside of us.

Hit the Gas!

1. Read Romans 8:12-17. How is God's personal emphasis made clear in this passage? Have you sensed that cry, 'Abba, Father,' in your own heart? How? _____

_____

_____

2. Do you have a sense of God's presence in your life? Are there times when his presence seems close, but other times when it seems distant? Why might this be? _____

_____

_____

THURSDAY

The Son of Thunder

"Like the time he told you about becoming like a little child? I always liked that story."

"Yes. That was a hard lesson," answered the old man. "We were all so cocky then, so proud. We thought we were going to take over the world."

"But you did!"

"Well, in so many words, yes; Jesus' Kingdom. But we didn't think of it that way then. I remember how we were all bickering—which was rather usual for us, I'm sorry to say. James and I continually fought to get the best spots at feasts, to sit next to Jesus. There was a group of women with children coming for his blessing; there were always so many in those days. And we tried to prevent them. I. . ."

Grandfather paused, and Israel detected the sadness in his voice.

"I even yelled at them several times. I say that to my shame. But Jesus had a way of getting his message across without being harsh about it. I loved that. It's so hard to confront people when they're wrong. But he simply drew one of the children to himself—a little girl as I recall, a beautiful child—and he told us that unless we became as a little child we wouldn't see the Kingdom of God. I'll tell you, that shut us up."

Grandfather chuckled, then continued. "Of course, then we fought over who was the most childlike in his faith! How foolish we were, even when we were with him."

"But you've changed since then."

"Yes. But there are so many things I wish I could be that he was."

"Like what?"

"Oh, gentle and firm at the same time. It's a difficult combination to master. You know what he called James and me, don't you?"

"The 'Sons of Thunder'!"

Grandfather laughed. "You say it the same way he did—with that twitch of a smile on his face, as if he found it amusing. And he did. He was always giving people new names."

"Oh?"

"Of course. Take Simon, for example. The first time Jesus met him he called him 'Peter.' It was his way of helping Simon understand that he intended to make us altogether different people. It was funny. Simon was often such a coward. But Jesus changed him."

"And you?"

"He called us the Sons of Thunder because we liked to thunder out lofty commands to everyone. We had a tendency to take over when Jesus wasn't there."

"I guess he was trying to tell you something."

"Yes, but in a friendly way. He never criticized us for our heavy-handedness. He only said he would transform it—turn that tendency into a spiritual strength."

"That's why you're such a great teacher."

Grandfather chuckled. "You think so? There are many who don't! But that was his way of loving people. He'd poke a little fun while making a point. And at the same time he'd tell you he respected you. Imagine that—being respected by the Lord of creation!"

Israel sat back and tried to imagine the scene. The Lord of creation! What an expression! But that was exactly what he was.

"I never quite thought of it that way," Israel said.

Grandfather patted Israel on the back. "There are many things he did which *I'd* never thought of!"

Pumpin' Premium

In *The World's Last Night*, C.S. Lewis wrote of a time when he got up early one morning so he could visit the barber in preparation for going to London. However, when the postman arrived, the first letter Lewis opened revealed that he didn't need to go to London that day. So he decided to skip the haircut.

Nonetheless, an impression in his heart said, "Get it cut all the same. Go and get it cut." Lewis fought off the impulse for a while, but in the end he gave in. His barber at that time was a fellow Christian and "a man of many troubles" that Lewis and his brother sometimes helped. It so happened that the moment Lewis walked into the barber shop, his friend exclaimed, "Oh, I was praying you might come today." It turned out Lewis was able to help him, and if he had come a day later he would have been of no help at all. Lewis concluded, "It awed me; it awes me still."

God's friendship with us is such that he is not only a friend to us, but a friend *through* us—to others.

Hit the Gas!

1. Look at Jesus' words in John 15:14-17. How is God's friendship shown to us according to these words? Do you feel as if Jesus has included you in a divine circle of friends to whom he has made known the things of the Father? _____

_____

_____

2. In what ways was Jesus a friend to the disciples? Name several that characterize your own relationship with him. _____

_____

_____

_____

FRIDAY

The Mother of Christ

"What other things impressed you about Jesus?" asked
Israel.

"Well, there were the many times he healed people without
them even asking. Many didn't know who he was. And some
were afraid to approach him. But he always reached out, even
when he knew they were afraid. He did that with me."

"Please tell me about that, Grandfather."

The old man was silent for a while. Israel waited patiently. It
was often this way, even in worship and teaching; he would
pause and think. But what he spoke next always meant a lot.
Israel wondered why Grandfather had never written anything
like Matthew and Luke and Paul had. Then Grandfather spoke.
"There were several times. But the most vivid one was at the
cross."

Israel could tell Grandfather's throat was tight. He decided
not to say anything.

"I was the only one who was there when he died. The others
had run. But I wasn't there because I was courageous. At first, I
ran, too."

Israel felt Grandfather's eyes on him. When Grandfather
didn't speak, Israel looked up. The old man's silver eyes were
fixed on him.

"And then Mary came and told me they were going to cruci-
fy him. She asked me to come with her. She always looked on me
as another son because I had spent so much time in her house. I
couldn't let her down, even though I had failed Jesus."

Grandfather's voice was husky. Israel listened intently.

"I thought Jesus wanted nothing more to do with me then. I felt as though this was the end—we'd all deserted him, and he no longer cared. Of course, there were so many things we didn't understand..."

Grandfather's voice broke. Israel had not seen him emotional often. He touched Grandfather's knee with his hand.

"As we stood there, I heard him say several things. I was numb, unable to speak. I wanted to ask his forgiveness for my cowardice. And then..."

Israel waited. Grandfather was silent for nearly a minute.

"Then he looked at me and Mary. His look was one of such compassion, even in his pain. And he said to Mary, 'Woman, behold your son!' He moved his head as though pointing to me. Then he said to me, 'Behold your mother.' It was a..."

Again Grandfather paused. Israel held his breath.

"It was a tender moment. But I knew then how much he loved Mary. And how much he loved..."

Israel looked into his grandfather's eyes. There were tears in the corners.

"...me. To entrust me with his own mother's care. It was almost beyond my ability to comprehend."

There was a long silence.

Pumpin' Premium

On the back of his book *Knowing God* (Intervarsity Press, 1973), J.I. Packer has a powerful series of questions and answers. They are:

What were we made for?
To know God.
What aim should we set ourselves in life?
To know God.
What is the eternal life that Jesus gives?

Knowledge of God.
What is the best thing in life?
Knowledge of God.
What in a man gives God most pleasure?
Knowledge of himself.

Perhaps I can add to it: What does God most want with us? A personal friendship, worship, and an eternal relationship—through which we will learn all there is to know of him.

That's a bit longer than Packer's succinct words, but such a relationship is what God longs to have with each of us. Jesus said in John 17:3, his last prayer for the church before his death, "And this is eternal life, that they may know Thee, the only true God, and Jesus Christ whom Thou hast sent."

Do you find yourself wanting to experience all there is of life? Then get to know God in Christ. Learn of him. Love him. Enjoy him. In him is life itself, life he came to give abundantly.

Hit the Gas!

1. Read what Jesus says in John 10:10. What is this life he came to give? Is Galatians 5:22-23 an adequate picture of that life? What other aspects of life do you think Christ came to give?

_____

_____

_____

2. What parts of Christ's life do you see active in your own life? What would you like him to bring into your life? Why? Can you pray about that now, asking him to develop those traits in you? _____

_____

_____

WEEKEND

He Was My Friend

Grandfather said, "I'll never forget that he loved me, Israel. I, one of the Sons of Thunder, a hard, exacting, prejudiced man. He loved me. Even today I don't understand it. Yes, Israel, He was my friend. The amazing thing is that he will be a friend like that to anyone who will believe."

Israel and Grandfather sat there watching the shadow of the fig tree by their house shiver in the slight breeze. Something puzzled Israel. He wasn't sure what it was.

Then suddenly he *did* know. "Grandfather, you must write it all down."

"Write what?"

"All of this. About Cana and Mary and Simon's nickname. No one else knows some of the things you saw with your own eyes. What if you die and these great truths die with you?"

Grandfather stared at Israel, his mouth open. "I never thought of that, Israel. I was never very good with letters. . ."

"But you can read and write. You *must* do it, Grandfather. So that all people will know about it, what he means to you."

Grandfather looked away down the street. Israel knew it was time to wait now. Nothing more could be said to this one whom he knew was a Son of Thunder still.

Finally, Grandfather rose. "Yes, I think you're right. God would have me do it. But I have one request."

"Yes?"

"That you will practice your own letters this way. I will speak what I know and you will write. Do you agree?"

"Nothing could please me more, Grandfather."

175

Pumpin' Premium

On February 11, 1861, Abraham Lincoln left his home in Springfield, Illinois and began the train journey to Washington, D.C., where he would be inaugurated as President. He bid a loving farewell from the rear of his train car platform. He ended his address with the words, "Today I leave you. I go to assume a task more difficult than that which devolved upon General Washington. The great God which guided him must help me. Without that assistance I shall surely fail; with it, I cannot fail."

In many ways, our nation has become what it is through faith like Lincoln's and that of many of our other leaders. A basic morality built on Scripture and Christian practices has been the basis of our laws, our outlook, and many of our traditions.

Now our nation is embroiled in a tremendous war of differing groups and philosophies. Never before has a Christian's faith been tested to this extreme in America. Today's Christians are the "bad guys," the wolverines, the ones all the interest groups and others battle for supremacy. What should we do as Christians? Do we wage political battle? Do we stage sit-ins and speak-ins and rallies supporting the issues we support and denouncing the laws we hate?

None of that is wrong. But ultimately, the thing that communicates to lost people is love—God's love poured through the simple hands and hearts of his people. It's that kind of enduring, caring, giving love that turns souls, one by one, to Christ.

John Wesley, the Christian evangelist who inflamed England in the early 1700s, once was traveling to a meeting in a carriage along a deeply rutted road. At one point, his carriage got stuck and he could make no headway. As helpers worked to get the carriage rolling again, a deeply distressed man came down the road. Wesley met him and asked him the cause of his anxiety. The man explained that a crop failure had left him destitute and in danger of losing his home because he couldn't pay the rent. He said, "The landlord is ready to turn us out, and I don't know where to go with my wife and children."

Wesley asked, "How much do you need?" The man answered that 20 shillings would clear his debt. Wesley smiled and took out his wallet. "I believe I can handle that," he said. "The Lord evidently wanted me to meet you." As the man left, happy and relieved, Wesley said, "Now I see why our carriage had to get stuck in the mud. Our steps were halted so that we might help that needy family."

James says that religion is worthless if we refuse to help those in need. "What use is it, my brethren, if a man says he has faith, but he has no works? Can that faith save him? If a brother or sister is without clothing and in need of daily food, and one of you says to them, 'Go in peace, be warmed and be filled,' and yet you do not give them what is necessary for their body, what use is that?" (James 2:14-16).

Jesus told the disciples that when the judgment comes, people will ask how they ministered to God. Christ would answer that when they visited the sick, clothed the naked, went to those in prison, and fed the hungry, they had literally done it to *him* (Matthew 25:31-46).

Knowing God, loving God, walking with Christ, and saying we live for him means little if we do not also love his people, whether saved or unsaved. That was one thing John learned from Jesus, his friend. It was exemplified by John Wesley with the man he met on the road. And it can be lived out by each of us simply by helping those in need, wherever we meet them.

As we do that, we will truly come to *enjoy* our fellowship with Christ. And that's exactly how he meant it to be.

Hit the Gas!

1. Read James 2:15-17. How can you apply this Scripture to your life today? _____

_____

_____

2. What steps can you take to enjoy Christ by enjoying his people? What avenues has he provided for you to do this?

_____

_____

_____

CONCLUSION

Let It Hum!

Years ago, I read in a devotional reader, *Our Daily Bread*, an illustration that has stuck with me. It's about a Wycliffe Bible translator in New Guinea who was struggling to translate a passage in Psalm 40: "I waited patiently for the Lord and he inclined to me and heard my cry" (40:1). He had difficulty with the word "inclined," because he knew of no word in the Guhu-Samane language that could be translated that way. He tried it several different ways, but nothing seemed to work.

Then one day, as he was walking through a village, he spotted a father who was holding his son on his knees. The boy strained upward to whisper into his father's ear. At the same time, the father turned his head sideways and leaned down, giving the child direct access to his left ear. Instantly, an idea occurred to the translator and he ran over, asking the man what he was doing as he listened to the lad. The father replied, "I'm spreading my ear out like a blanket."

That was all he needed. Immediately, the translator went home, picked up his pen, and translated the passage, "I continued to wait for the Lord, and he spread out his ear like a blanket. Hearing my cry, he drew me out of the mud and water and out of the fierce pit, and he placed my foot on a stone."

I often think of that image as I imagine myself talking and praying to God through Jesus. I can see him "spreading his ear out like a blanket" as he bends down to listen to me—little me.

I mean that sincerely. The greatest revelation that occurred to me the weekend that I became a Christian was the realization that I knew God, the Creator of the universe, the Lord and Potentate of

179

the Galaxies, the Master who had fashioned me in my mother's womb. He was my personal friend, someone who would be with me and would go with me everywhere I went.

Even today that realization startles me. Isn't it arrogant to say, "I know God. Jesus is my brother, Lord, and friend"? Aren't people insulted when we make such claims?

Some are. Indeed, many people revile Christianity because people have taken a lot of the majesty out of worship by making God personal. But that's what God wants—a relationship, a friendship, a closeness, an intimacy that will last for eternity.

What should our response to that reality be? I can only answer with a famed verse of Scripture: "As the deer pants for the water brooks, so my soul pants for Thee, O God" (Psalm 42:1).

Can you see that deer—frantic with thirst, darting through the forest running this way and that way on a hint of a scent? Water! Water!!!! WATER!!!!!!

And we might imagine ourselves saying, "God! God!!! GOD!!! I want to know you as completely as you can be known!"

That's the prayer of my heart. And it's the key to *Fillin' UP*.

Are you with me?